HAMLET

William Shakespeare

Edited by
CEDRIC WATTS

WORDSWORTH CLASSICS

For my husband
ANTHONY JOHN RANSON
with love from your wife, the publisher.
Eternally grateful for your unconditional love.

Readers who are interested in other titles from
Wordsworth Editions are invited to visit our website at
www.wordsworth-editions.com

First published in 1992 by Wordsworth Editions Limited
8B East Street, Ware, Hertfordshire SG12 9HJ

ISBN 978 1 85326 009 4

Text © Wordsworth Editions Limited 2002
Introduction, notes and other editorial matter © Cedric Watts 2002

Wordsworth® is a registered trademark of
Wordsworth Editions Limited

Wordsworth Editions
is the company founded in 1987 by
MICHAEL TRAYLER

Typeset in Great Britain by Antony Gray
Printed and bound by Clays Ltd, Elcograf S.p.A.

CONTENTS

GENERAL INTRODUCTION

The Wordsworth Classics' Shakespeare Series, with *Romeo and Juliet*, *Henry V* and *The Merchant of Venice* as its inaugural volumes, presents a newly-edited sequence of William Shakespeare's works. Wordsworth Classics are inexpensive paperbacks for students and for the general reader. Each play in the Shakespeare Series is accompanied by a standard apparatus, including an introduction, explanatory notes and a glossary. The textual editing takes account of recent scholarship while giving the material a careful reappraisal. The apparatus is, however, concise rather than elaborate. We hope that the resultant volumes prove to be handy, reliable and helpful. Above all, we hope that, from Shakespeare's works, readers will derive pleasure, wisdom, provocation, challenges, and insights: insights into his culture and ours, and into the era of civilisation to which his writings have made – and continue to make – such potently influential contributions. Shakespeare's eloquence will, undoubtedly, re-echo 'in states unborn and accents yet unknown'.

CEDRIC WATTS
Series Editor

INTRODUCTION

I

Shakespeare's *Hamlet* is probably the most famously problematic play ever written. Wherever you look, it seems to offer problems, big, medium and small. The early texts vary greatly: which, if any, is authoritative? The religious and moral implications of the play seem inconsistent. The Ghost is strikingly ambiguous. Why is the historical setting both ancient and modern? Why is Horatio both informed and uninformed about Danish matters? Was Claudius's marriage to Gertrude really incestuous? As for Hamlet himself: why does he delay? How mad is he? Why does he treat Ophelia so badly? Why does the text specify that he's thirty years old, even though he's still a student? Why does he profess uncertainty of what lies beyond death, even though he has spoken to a ghost? What is the key to his character? Thus the questions multiply. For centuries, commentators have wrangled about them. The play's pregnancy breeds midwives.

What keeps the wrangles going is largely the following combinations of factors. First, there are commentators who hope to find a play as unified and intelligible as possible, and who tend to treat this play as text rather than as performance. Secondly, parts of *Hamlet* give evidence of a lack of intelligent co-ordination; there are even signs of confusion or contradiction. Thirdly, much of *Hamlet* displays splendidly intelligent co-ordination: incisive ironies, subtle thematic connections, telling dramatic contrasts. Fourthly, some parts have an uncertain status, so that commentators will argue about whether they are intelligently integrated or not. Similarly, the characterisation of Hamlet himself includes features which are well co-ordinated and features which are contradictory or perplexing;

and, of course, his character has an opaque area which is made conspicuous (or generated) by his declared perplexity concerning its content. Hamlet says: 'I do not know / Why yet I live to say "This thing's to do" ': so we are seduced into seeking an answer for him. 'You would pluck out the heart of my mystery', he scornfully declares, and thus challenges us to be mystery-solvers.

Some commentators, notably the influential A. C. Bradley and the Freudian Ernest Jones, produced interpretations which emphasised the intelligent co-ordination of the work. For Bradley, the key to the central character and to much of the play was provided by Hamlet's nature: Gertrude's re-marriage provided a 'violent shock to his moral being' which caused him to 'sink into melancholy': hence Hamlet's morbid brooding and incapacity for action.[1] For Ernest Jones, the key to the character and the play was the Freudian 'Oedipus Complex': this explained both the delay and Hamlet's bafflement. According to Jones's theory, the explanation of Hamlet's reluctance to kill Claudius is that Claudius (by killing Hamlet's father and marrying his mother) has enacted the Prince's own repressed desires; but, precisely because these desires *are* repressed, Hamlet cannot understand his own delay.[2] In contrast to such 'co-ordinating' interpreters, other commentators, and most famously T. S. Eliot, argued that the play was radically disunited. Eliot declared *Hamlet* so incoherent as to be 'most certainly an artistic failure': 'probably more people have thought *Hamlet* a work of art because they found it interesting, than have found it interesting because it is a work of art'; 'Shakespeare tackled a problem which proved too much for him'.[3]

Accordingly, Part 2 of this Introduction presents the case of someone who wishes to emphasise the puzzles, gaps and apparent inconsistencies of the play. Part 3 offers a contrasting case. Finally, Part 4 attempts to adjudicate.

2

The most fundamental problem is the inconsistency of the textual bases of the play. The foundation of all subsequent editions is provided by the three earliest texts: the First Quarto of 1603, the Second Quarto of 1604–5, and the First Folio of 1623. (Very roughly, a 'quarto' is a book with relatively small pages, and a 'folio' is a book with large pages.)[4] They differ greatly from each other. A common practice of modern editors is to construct a new text of *Hamlet*, taking as the basis the Second Quarto, while adding bits and pieces from the later First Folio and smaller bits from the First Quarto, and then modernising, in varying degrees, the spelling, punctuation and stage-directions (often adding new stage-directions); and, where the text seems obscure or garbled, they offer their own attempts at clarification, or copy previous editorial attempts. Other editors may take as basis the First Folio instead of the Second Quarto, while following the same general procedure. The editors thus seek to create an ample, co-ordinated text of high quality. That endeavour is understandable and worthwhile; but it may create the illusion of a fixed, finished, stable text, and may mask the variety and variability of the original materials. If you look up those early versions, the First Quarto, Second Quarto and First Folio (which have been variously reproduced in facsimile form), you find that what you are looking at is not so much *The Tragical History of Hamlet, Prince of Denmark* as *The Evolving Hamlet-Material for the Use of Players*.[5]

The original texts, in all their discrepancies and divergences, show that in Shakespeare's day the script of *Hamlet* was a pliable body of material, moving through time and changing as it moved, growing here, shrinking there, being revised and tinkered with, doubtless by Shakespeare, probably by his fellow-actors, and eventually by printers. That material may well have been performed in different ways at different locations. The short version leaves room for embellishments, while the long versions provide plenty of scope for cutting. The First Quarto's title-page claims that the play was performed at Oxford and Cambridge, as well as London. In 1608 *Hamlet* was staged at sea by the crew of Captain Keeling's ship *Dragon*, so that the men would not waste their time on 'idlenes[s] and unlawful games, or sleepe'; doubtless this performance differed considerably from those staged at Court.[6] Though *Hamlet* has been very popular on stage ever since Shakespeare's day, the play is hardly ever performed in full. Some of the characters may vanish completely. Directors often eliminate Fortinbras, which considerably depletes the play's political significance; and Reynaldo, Voltemand and Cornelius may also join him in oblivion.

In addition to the textual discrepancies, there are various apparent contradictions within the play which suggest that Shakespeare worked by trial and error, first thoughts being overtaken by second thoughts. He may never have reached the point at which he could say: 'This is the final, perfected version of the script.' One apparent contradiction is that when Hamlet has the bright idea of arranging a play at court to test Claudius, the idea arrives twice instead of once. In the soliloquy at the end of Act 2, scene 2 (in our edition), we see him conceiving the plan, and there he seems quite unaware that he has already – in the same scene – asked the First Player to perform *The Murder of Gonzago* (or *The Mousetrap*) with his own special additions. Again, another contradiction may be that Fortinbras is depicted initially as an impetuous hot-head leading a gang of lawless adventurers, even though later he will be depicted as a statesman-like commander worthy of inheriting the Danish throne (having received Hamlet's vote). A further problem is that Horatio seems to be not only a resident, familiar with Danish politics and able to explain the political situation to the sentries, but also a visitor who has to have the Danish custom of drunken carousals explained to him by Hamlet. Is he an insider or an outsider? Then there's the famous problem of Hamlet's age. Hamlet is a student at Wittenberg University, as is Horatio; and, for much of the time, we have the impression that Hamlet is about nineteen or twenty, and Horatio a year or two older. Yet, in Act 5, scene 1, the grave-digger specifies that Hamlet is thirty, which clashes with our sense of his youthful idealism, moodiness and impetuosity. It is tempting to speculate that what the play offers there is a compromise between Shakespeare's original conception of the character and the evident age of the actor of the part. The play was first performed around 1600. The part of Hamlet was played by Richard Burbage, and he was probably over thirty years old at the time: reference-books give his date of birth as *circa* 1568.[7] During the duel scene, Burbage might well have been 'fat and scant of breath' (sweaty – or perhaps overweight – and panting), as the text declares.

There is a peculiar cluster of problems around the Ghost. Arguably, the Ghost is both awe-inspiring and ludicrous. The apparition certainly inspires awe and fear in the sentries and even in Horatio; but, equally, in the peculiarly protracted scene of swearing to secrecy, the Ghost seems to become a ludicrous butt of Hamlet's humour: he becomes for a while the 'old mole', the 'worthy pioner' (or sapper) and even 'this fellow in the cellarage' – so that briefly the awe-inspiring apparition dwindles into the embarrassed actor scuttling about in the dusty gloom under the planks of the Elizabethan stage. That word 'cellarage' suggests the dark under-stage area, rather than the lofty battlements of Elsinore Castle. A subtler problem is that of the Ghost's provenance. Is he indeed a spirit from Purgatory, as he claims, or is he a devil in disguise?[8] When Hamlet stages the play of *The Mousetrap*, its prime function is to test the Ghost; for, if Claudius manifests guilt, this will prove that the apparition is truthful – that he is an 'honest ghost'. Claudius does indeed manifest guilt; so, for most of us, the mystery about the Ghost seems to be resolved. Banquo in *Macbeth* reminds us, however, that the Devil and his agents can tell the truth when it serves their evil purposes. As Banquo says: 'And oftentimes, to win us to our harm, / The instruments of darkness tell us truths'. Thus, even if the Ghost is right about Claudius, that does not prove that the apparition is trustworthy. In Shakespeare's plays, ghosts usually do have the identities that they claim, and this apparition does indeed sound convincingly like the former warrior-king of Denmark; therefore, most of us, probably, assume that his excursion from Purgatory manifests a divine purpose. But then an obvious contradiction appears. This Ghost (who, by confirming the existence of Purgatory, confirms the existence of Heaven, Hell and – of course – the God of Christianity) orders Prince Hamlet to complete a specifically anti-Christian task: that of bloody revenge, which the God of both the Old Testament and the New Testament explicitly forbids: 'Thou shalt not kill'; 'Vengeance is mine, I will repay, saith the Lord'.[9] Theologically, the play is riven with contradictions. The student from Wittenberg (a centre of Protestantism in the sixteenth century) encounters a ghost who claims to come from the Purgatory specified by Catholicism; yet this same student terms the region after death 'The undiscovered country, from whose bourn / No traveller returns', even though he has recently talked to an apparition who purports to be a traveller returning from that country. Hamlet says he hopes to kill Claudius in circumstances which will ensure that Claudius goes to Hell; nevertheless, this very believer elsewhere expresses the radically sceptical notion that 'there is nothing either good or bad, but thinking makes it so'.

The Ghost was indignant about Gertrude's incest with Claudius. The laws of the Church (following Leviticus 18:16 and 20:21) expressly forbade a man to marry a widowed sister-in-law. Hamlet, too, seems appalled by the act of incest; indeed, he seems more disgusted by the incestuous sexuality than by the poisoning of his father. The difficulty here is that although the murder was secret, the marriage of Claudius to Gertrude was public and ceremonial; yet, apart from Hamlet and the Ghost, nobody seems to have noticed anything incestuous about it. Nor can this be taken as evidence that the court is sexually decadent, for the early conversations between Ophelia, Laertes and Polonius suggest that, in sexual matters, this court is conventionally respectable in its morality. Perhaps an ecclesiastical dispensation was provided for Claudius (as it was provided for Henry VIII when he married Catherine of Aragon, widow of his brother Arthur), but the play doesn't say so.[10] Once again, the gaps in the play solicit us to provide gap-filling (and possibly distorting) speculations.

This brings us back to Hamlet's character. He dominates the play, so that the cliché 'Hamlet without the Prince' is a byword for absurdity. If Hamlet's character is incoherent, the play is incoherent. In 1931, A. J. A. Waldock, in *Hamlet: A Study in Critical Method*, offered the following argument. *Hamlet*, the play, is a palimpsest: new material has been superimposed on old, and the old shows through with confusing effect.[11] All the main problems of the play may stem from the fact that sophisticated Shakespeare was working on primitive materials. The original story of Hamlet (or Amlothi, or Amleth, as he was called) belonged to the harsh Dark Ages, the era of pagan Nordic sagas. It was transmitted to Shakespeare from mediaeval Scandinavia via Saxo Grammaticus's *Historiae Danicae*, written around AD 1200, via the *Histoires Tragiques* of Belleforest (*circa* 1570), and via a lost play by Thomas Kyd (*circa* 1590); and Shakespeare did what he could to modernise the legend and make it more subtle, sensitive and realistic. But, it can be argued, too much of the old barbaric plot and of the old crude Amleth remain; and the result is inconsistency. Hamlet himself is a hybrid because he is partly a modern philosopher and partly a primitive avenger. His motivation is largely inherited and literary: he does certain things because they are what the legendary Amleth traditionally did. The feigned madness, the murder of an

It is a doctrine which reconciles chance and destiny, muddle and structure. Implicitly, it redeems much that may seem digressive or anomalous in the play.

Another sign of highly intelligent and richly ironic co-ordination by Shakespeare is the multiplication of avengers. In the source-story, there is just one son seeking revenge for a slain father: that son is Amleth himself. In Shakespeare's play, we find not just one son seeking revenge for a slain father, but four sons. In addition to Hamlet, there are young Fortinbras, Laertes and Pyrrhus. The First Player's long recitation tells how the Trojan king, old Priam, was hacked to pieces by the Greek warrior Pyrrhus, who was avenging his slain father, Achilles. The Prince never says that revenge is wrong, and he usually talks as though it is right; but, when you consider the ironic connections and differences between these four avengers, Hamlet, Fortinbras, Laertes and Pyrrhus, you find that the ethic of revenge has received a very thorough and very critical examination. The player's recitation evokes pity for the slain Priam and his grief-stricken wife, Hecuba, and depicts the avenging Pyrrhus as a gory monster. The characterisation of Laertes, who is impetuous in his desire for revenge and says that he would willingly cut Hamlet's throat in a church, makes us look the more sympathetically on the procrastinating Hamlet who had refrained from murdering Claudius at prayer; and it strengthens the idea that when Hamlet spared Claudius then, saying that he preferred to kill him in circumstances to ensure his damnation, that was really a ration-alisation of delay rather than a Machiavellian intention. Some confirmation of this is provided by the marked ambiguity of Hamlet's professed admiration for the Fortinbras who, after being deflected from a vengeful attack on Denmark, leads his army to battle in Poland for 'a little patch of ground / That hath in it no profit but the name.' The more Hamlet says how noble it is to 'find quarrel in a straw' and to expose what is mortal and unsure 'To all that fortune, death and danger dare, / Even for an egg-shell', the more his own phrasing ('quarrel in a *straw*', 'Even for an *egg-shell*') enables us to hear an undercurrent of scepticism about the value of such lethal honour. Repeatedly, it's that tinge of scepticism in Hamlet's reflections which gives them a curiously modern quality. Hamlet is a character who seems to be reaching forward intellectually to later eras: indeed, he's helping to generate those later eras of thought: helping to propagate a very modern kind of personality which can establish a critical (and even alienating) distance between itself and its ideological environment.

Thus, when we look back on this quartet of vengeful sons, we see that it creates a strong thematic patterning: the ethic of revenge and the nature of virile 'honour' receive close scrutiny. We then may see that the play is co-ordinated by many such interwoven themes. These themes include the following: actors, acting and action; action versus reflection; mousetraps of various kinds (Claudius being caught in his own trap); attitudes to death; 'appetite' as simultaneously ambition. lust and intemperance; conflict between the older and the younger generations; women as victims of male violence (for Ophelia, Gertrude and Hecuba are all victims of that violence); melancholia and madness; and man as both Hyperion and satyr, both paragon of animals and quintessence of dust. Again and again, the play looks over the edge of life into death, and it offers contrasting vistas of the region: seeing unquiet slumbers, Purgatory, flights of heaven-bound angels, politic worms, and the transmutation of Caesar into clay. But the persistent questioning is a major co-ordinator. Indeed, the sense of the questioning of appearances is established in the play's very first words: 'Who's there?' / 'Nay, answer *me*. Stand and unfold yourself.' Thus, by repeatedly questioning the obvious and subverting the conventional, Shakespeare has converted the material of a mere revenge drama into a tragedy. He has provided the ethical complexity which, for modern audiences and critics, is one of the defining characteristics of the tradition of tragedy.

If there be any doubt that Shakespeare's imagination is shrewdly in control, consider the following details. Polonius tells the Prince that he, Polonius, had once played the part of Julius Caesar and was stabbed to death by Brutus. 'It was a brute part of him', puns Hamlet (i.e. 'That was a brutish act for the acted Brutus'). This reference foreshadows the brutal stabbing of Polonius by the Prince. Fiction portends fact.[13] A second, related detail concerns the players who come to court. They have been obliged to go on tour because, in the city, juvenile actors have become popular. Hamlet himself makes the thematic connection with events at Elsinore:

It is not very strange; for my uncle is King of Denmark, and those that would make mouths at him while my father lived, give twenty, forty, fifty, a hundred ducats apiece for his picture in little.

In both cases, in Hamlet's view, the unworthy has displaced the worthy, and unreasoning adulation has been accorded. There is, in addition, a more obvious thematic function here. The players emphasise the theme of actors, acting and action. 'Acting' can mean 'playing a part' or 'pretending to be what you are not'. Claudius is a usurper playing the part of a rightful king. Hamlet reflects that the Ghost may be a devil playing the part of King Hamlet. The Prince asks Horatio and the sentries not to reveal the truth if he should act in a deranged manner. And when central figures are performing rôles, the theme of 'spying, eavesdropping and testing' is entailed. Ghost, Claudius, Polonius, Rosencrantz and Guildenstern spy on Hamlet; he, in various ways, spies on them; and his own recessive inner nature seems to elude fully-focused perception by himself or anyone else. Furthermore, 'acting' can mean 'undertaking and fulfilling a course of action, instead of passively reflecting or talking (or giving time-consuming "performances")': so it could be said that Hamlet is divided by the two conflicting senses of that verb.

Other telling details are found in the duel scene. In Act 1, near the play's opening, we heard the noise of drum, trumpets and cannon which accompanied the festive carousals at the celebrations not only of the marriage of Gertrude and Claudius but also of Hamlet's apparent reconciliation with the couple. In Act 5, near the play's conclusion, we again hear drumming, trumpeting and cannonades, now accompanying the festive carousals at the duel which will result in the deaths of Gertrude and Claudius – and of Hamlet himself. The sound-effects provide symmetrical ceremonial irony. When Hamlet presses the poisoned cup to the lips of Claudius, he says: 'Is thy union here?'; and that word 'union' connotes, all at once, the pearl, the poison, and the reunion of Claudius with Gertrude in the night of death. No wonder that the French duelling master who had inspired Claudius to initiate the duel bears the name Lamord, equivalent to La Mort – Death.

4

In Part 2, I summarised the case of someone who seeks to argue that the play is a muddle. In Part 3, I summarised the case of someone who seeks to argue that it is well organised. You can guess what Part 4 says. They're both right, up to a point; and both wrong, in their over-valuation of textual unity. Thematic scansion of a text, emphasised in Part 3, always tends to unify a work in our imagination; that's because themes are very pliable and elastic. On the other hand, a more technical and inquisitorial scansion of a text, testing detail against detail for logical consistency, generally reveals tensions and contradictions – particularly when we are looking at Elizabethan and Jacobean material. My main point is that it's the friction between those two viewpoints, both dominated by the notion of the desirability of rational unity in the printed text, that has generated so much of the debate about Shakespeare's *Hamlet* and its central character. Step back from the text and think of the play as material to be performed, and the perspective changes. Largely as a consequence of its combination of brilliant order and puzzling disorder, of design and muddle, of plenitude and lacunae, this tragedy has been, and remains, astonishingly successful in the theatre. What is troublesome for the scholar – the inconsistency and unreliability of the early texts, the gaps or inconsistencies in the edited play – is joy for the directors, actors and their audiences. There's so much to be done with this play. It's full of vitality and diversity: there's comedy in it, tragedy and pathos, the cynical and the sentimental; elements of the grotesque and of savage farce; the philosophical range; the telling images (Hamlet with the skull; a usurping king flinching from a player-king); there's the spectacular violence, the scathing sexual frankness ('the rank sweat of an enseamèd bed', 'honeying and making love / Over the nasty sty') and the cruelty ('Get thee to a nunnery'); yet there's the subtlety, the urbanity and the magnanimity. The modern is emerging strikingly from the Mediaeval and the Elizabethan. The play is packed with now-famous epitomes and maxims ('[T]o thine own self be true'; 'To be, or not to be'; 'What a piece of work is a man: how noble in reason, how infinite in faculties'; 'Alas, poor Yorick . . . '; '[T]he rest is silence'): indeed, one of the challenges for a director is to save the play from sounding like an anthology of familiar quotations, and thus to let it emerge clearly from the dazzling aureole of its own fame. It's not surprising that actors queue for the rôle of Hamlet ('the part has become a hoop through which aspiring classical actors have to jump', said Derek Jacobi).[14] The Prince himself is actor, director and literary critic combined. He recites from memory a long passage describing Pyrrhus; he shrewdly mimics the styles of Polonius, Laertes and Osric; and his wit probes affectation and insincerity wherever he encounters it. Indeed, his wit is almost obsessive: character after character becomes a stooge for it: not only Claudius, Polonius, Rosencrantz, Guildenstern and Osric, but even the Ghost. Hamlet is a virtuoso soliciting virtuosi: the part tests the full range of the actor's voice and physique; yet at the same time the characterisation has its mysteries and reticences, so there's always something new to be contributed in performance. Feminists know that the part has attracted great actresses too. Prince Hamlet has been played by, for example, Sarah Siddons, Charlotte Cushman, Millicent Bandemann-Palmer, Sarah Bernhardt and Asta Nielsen: an apt cultural riposte, given that Gertrude and Ophelia were originally played by boys. Hamlet has even been performed by a pair of twins simultaneously: Anthony and David Meyer. All this forms a tribute to Shakespeare's brilliance in creating a character who is not only complex, not only adroitly intelligent and mercurially active, but also (avowedly) a mystery to himself, so that mystery-solving interpretations are constantly being offered. Hamlet thus resembles Proteus, the god who eluded capture by incessantly changing shape. As Jonathan Miller has said:

> We will never be, and no one has ever been, introduced to Hamlet. I think of Hamlet as a series of lines [at] which an infinite series of claimants arrives . . . [15]

Furthermore, the play is exceptional in the scope that it provides for directors. If the early texts are so diverse (and two of them are so lengthy), directors have abundant opportunities for shaping and re-shaping the material by means of cuts, compressions and transpositions. The director is unusually free to make a living play, a new temporary unity, out of the raw materials provided by the author and by the others involved in the production of the texts. *Hamlet* was evidently, in Shakespeare's time, an evolving work, and it has continued to evolve since then, shifting and changing in response to diverse cultural needs and pressures. Of course, Shakespeare would have approved of directorial pruning and even directorial additions to the text. He took ample liberties with his sources. Hamlet is delighted to add lines to *The Mousetrap* to give it topical relevance; and when Polonius objects that the recitation about Pyrrhus is too long, Hamlet immediately replies: 'It shall to the barber's, with your beard.' There may be no Platonically-ideal *Hamlet* text to be discovered by scholarly scrutiny of the words on the page; but innumerable living *Hamlet*s can be generated on stage, on screen, and in the imaginations of audiences and readers down the ages.

CEDRIC WATTS

NOTES TO THE INTRODUCTION

1 A. C. Bradley: *Shakespearean Tragedy* [1904] (London: Macmillan, 1957), p. 93.

2 Ernest Jones: *Hamlet and Oedipus* (London: Gollancz, 1949), esp. pp. 90–1.

3 T. S. Eliot: 'Hamlet' [1919] in *Selected Essays* (London: Faber and Faber, 1932; rpt. 1963), pp. 143, 144 and 146.

4 More precisely: a quarto is a book consisting of clusters of leaves, each cluster produced by folding a sheet of paper twice so as to make four leaves (eight pages). In a folio, each sheet has been folded once so as to make two leaves (four pages).

5 The clearest basis for comparison is provided in *The Three-Text Hamlet: Parallel Texts of the First and Second Quartos and First Folio*, ed. Paul Bertram and Bernice W. Kliman (New York: AMS Press, 1991).

6 See E. K Chambers: *William Shakespeare: A Study of Facts and Problems* (London: Oxford University Press, 1930, reprinted 1951), Vol. II, pp. 335 (the *Dragon* production), 346 (possible performance at court *c*.1619–20), 353 (performance for the King and Queen at Hampton Court in 1637).

7 See, for example, F. E. Halliday's *A Shakespeare Companion* (Harmonds-worth: Penguin, 1964), p. 77. Laurence Olivier was forty when making his film of *Hamlet* (released in 1948).

8 A detailed exposition of the view that the Ghost is diabolical can be found in Eleanor Prosser's *Hamlet and Revenge* (London: Oxford University Press, 1967).

9 See Exodus 20:13, Matthew 5:21 and 5:44, Deuteronomy 32:35 and Romans 12:19.

10 In *Fratricide Punished* (a translation of *Der bestrafte Brudermord*, a German version of the play), the Queen says: 'Had not the Pope allowed such a marriage, it would never have happened.'

11 'The old material seems here and there to bulge out awkwardly into the new play', says Waldock. See *Hamlet: A Study in Critical Method* (Cambridge: Cambridge University Press, 1931), p. 66.

12 'An Essay on Man', I, 290, in *The Poems of Alexander Pope*, ed. John Butt (London: Methuen, 1963), p. 515.

13 In *Hamlet*, ed. Harold Jenkins (London: Methuen, 1982), p. 294, the editor remarks:

It is likely enough that the roles of Caesar and Brutus in *Caes.* (first performed 1599) were taken by the same actors as now played Polonius and Hamlet; so that 'Hamlet' would already have killed 'Polonius' in a previous play . . .

14 Jacobi is quoted in *Shakespeare in Perspective*, Vol. 1 (London: Ariel Books, 1982), p. 191.

15 Miller is quoted in Ralph Berry's *On Directing Shakespeare* (London: Croom Helm; New York: Barnes and Noble, 1977), p. 38.

FURTHER READING
(in chronological order)

A. C. Bradley: *Shakespearean Tragedy* [1904]. Basingstoke: Macmillan, 1992.

T. S. Eliot: 'Hamlet' [1919] in *Selected Essays*. London: Faber and Faber, 1932; enlarged edition, 1951.

G. Wilson Knight: 'The Embassy of Death: An Essay on *Hamlet*' in *The Wheel of Fire* [1930]. London: Methuen, 1986.

A. J. A. Waldock: *Hamlet: A Study in Critical Method*. Cambridge: Cambridge University Press, 1931.

Ernest Jones: *Hamlet and Oedipus*. London: Gollancz, 1949.

Raymond Mander and Joe Mitchenson: *Hamlet through the Ages*. London: Rockliff, 1952.

Fredson Bowers: *Elizabethan Revenge Tragedy, 1587–1642*. Gloucester, Mass.: Smith, 1959.

F. E. Halliday: *A Shakespeare Companion 1564–1964*. Harmondsworth: Penguin, 1964.

Shakespeare: Hamlet: A Casebook, ed. John Jump. London: Macmillan, 1968.

Twentieth Century Interpretations of 'Hamlet': A Collection of Critical Essays, ed. David Bevington. Englewood Cliffs, N.J.: Prentice-Hall, 1968.

Narrative and Dramatic Sources of Shakespeare, Vol. 7, ed. Geoffrey Bullough. London: Routledge & Kegan Paul; New York: Columbia University Press; 1973.

Ralph Berry: *On Directing Shakespeare*. London: Croom Helm, 1977.

Samuel Schoenbaum: *William Shakespeare: A Compact Documentary Life*. London and New York: Oxford University Press, 1977; reprinted, 1987.

Martin Scofield: *The Ghosts of Hamlet: The Play and Modern Writers*. Cambridge: Cambridge University Press, 1980.

Peter Davison: *Hamlet: Text and Performance*. Houndmills and London: Macmillan, 1983.

The Cambridge Companion to Shakespeare Studies, ed. Stanley Wells. Cambridge: Cambridge University Press, 1986.

William Empson: *Essays on Shakespeare*, ed. David B. Pirie. Cambridge: Cambridge University Press, 1986.

G. R. Hibbard: 'General Introduction' and 'Textual Introduction': *Hamlet*. Oxford: Oxford University Press, 1987.

Bernice W. Kliman: *Hamlet: Film, Television and Audio Performance*. Cranbury, N. J.: Associated University Presses, 1988.

Cedric Watts: *Hamlet*. Hemel Hempstead: Harvester Wheatsheaf; Boston: Twayne; 1988.

The Three-Text Hamlet, ed. Paul Bertram and Bernice W. Kliman. New York: AMS Press, 1991.

Janet Adelman: *Suffocating Mothers: Fantasies of Maternal Origin in Shakespeare's Plays, 'Hamlet' to 'The Tempest'*. New York and London: Routledge, 1992.

M. M. Mahood: *Bit Parts in Shakespeare's Plays*. Cambridge: Cambridge University Press, 1992.

Russ McDonald: *The Bedford Companion to Shakespeare*. New York: St Martin's Press; Basingstoke: Macmillan; 1996.

Richard Corum: *Understanding 'Hamlet': A Student Casebook for Issues, Sources, and Historical Documents*. Westport, Conn.: Greenwood Press, 1998.

Kenneth S. Rothwell: *Shakespeare on Screen: A Century of Film and Television*. Cambridge: Cambridge University Press, 1999.

John Sutherland and Cedric Watts: *Henry V, War Criminal? and Other Shakespeare Puzzles*. Oxford: Oxford University Press, 2000.

NOTE ON SHAKESPEARE

Details of Shakespeare's early life are scanty. He was the son of a prosperous merchant of Stratford-upon-Avon, and tradition gives his date of birth as 23 April, 1564; certainly, three days later, he was christened at the parish church. It is likely that he attended the local Grammar School but had no university education. Of his early career there is no record, though John Aubrey states that he was a country schoolmaster. In 1582 Shakespeare married Anne Hathaway, with whom he had two daughters, Susanna and Judith, and a son, Hamnet, who died in 1596. How he became involved with the stage in London is uncertain, but he was sufficiently established as a playwright by 1592 to be criticised in print as a challengingly versatile 'upstart Crow'. He was a leading member of the Lord Chamberlain's company, which became the King's Men on the accession of James I in 1603. Being not only a playwright and actor but also a 'sharer' (one of the owners of the company, entitled to a share of the profits), Shakespeare prospered greatly, as is proven by the numerous records of his financial transactions. Towards the end of his life, he loosened his ties with London and retired to New Place, the large house in Stratford which he had bought in 1597. He died on 23 April, 1616, and is buried in the place of his baptism, Holy Trinity Church. The earliest collected edition of his plays, the First Folio, was published in 1623, and its prefatory verse-tributes include Ben Jonson's famous declaration, 'He was not of an age, but for all time'.

ACKNOWLEDGEMENTS AND TEXTUAL MATTERS

With a title like that, this section may seem skippable; but the textual comments could be useful if you have to write an essay on *Hamlet*, or if you face an examination-question about it, or if you are involved in a production of the play. The gist of the matter is that, from Shakespeare's day to the present, the text has been strikingly and fruitfully variable, and will long remain so.

I have consulted, and am indebted to, numerous editions of *Hamlet*, notably those by: Horace Howard Furness (1877; reprinted, New York: Dover, 1963); G. L. Kittredge (Boston: Ginn, 1939); John Dover Wilson (London: Cambridge University Press, 1958); Cyrus Hoy (New York: Norton, 1963; 2nd edn., 1992); G. Blakemore Evans *et al.* (*The Riverside Shakespeare*: Boston, Mass.: Houghton Mifflin, 1974); Harold Jenkins (the Arden Shakespeare: London, Methuen, 1982); Philip Edwards (Cambridge: Cambridge University Press, 1985); G. R. Hibbard (Oxford: Oxford University Press, 1987; reprinted, 1998); Paul Bertram and Bernice Kliman (*The Three-Text Hamlet*: New York: AMS Press, 1991); Graham Holderness and Bryan Loughrey (Hemel Hempstead: Harvester Wheatsheaf, 1992); and Stephen Greenblatt *et al.* (*The Norton Shakespeare*: New York and London: Norton, 1997). The Glossary adapts that of John Dover Wilson, which I have revised by reference to the *Oxford English Dictionary* and to recent editions of the play. I am grateful for the textual advice of J. M. Glauser.

In 1602, *Hamlet* was registered as a play 'lately Acted' by the Lord Chamberlain's Men. In the following year appeared the First Quarto (Q1). This offers a short – and often apparently garbled – text of the play. It has 2,154 lines,[1] and many of the speeches seem to be rather clumsy versions. A standard illustration is the 'To be, or not to be' soliloquy. In its customary form, it opens like this:

> To be, or not to be: that is the question:
> Whether 'tis nobler in the mind to suffer
> The slings and arrow of outrageous fortune,
> Or to take arms against a sea of troubles,
> And, by opposing, end them. To die – to sleep,

No more; and by a sleep to say we end
The heart-ache and the thousand natural shocks
That flesh is heir to: 'tis a consummation
Devoutly to be wished. To die, to sleep;
To sleep, perchance to dream. Ay, there's the rub . . .

In the First Quarto, however, what Hamlet says is this:

To be, or not to be, I there's the point,
To Die, to sleepe, is that all? I all:
No, to sleepe, to dreame, I mary there it goes . . .

Markedly different: the Q1 Hamlet sounds less composed and more
hasty and dithery; or perhaps someone other than Shakespeare is
drastically summarising (with damage to the metre) some ill-
remembered lines. One widely-accepted explanation of such
differences is that this so-called 'Bad Quarto' is memorially assem-
bled. The argument has various forms, but a favoured form is that
the actor who played both Marcellus and Lucianus reconstructed
the play from memory (perhaps aided by notes) and eventually sold
the material to a printer.[2] The brevity of this text may result partly
from lapses of memory and partly from the possibility that the play
being recalled was itself shorter – perhaps abridged – and rather
different (Polonius being there 'Corambis', while Reynaldo was
'Montano') at that point in its evolution.[3] Even though Q1 often
seems rough and unreliable, it contains interesting material lacking
from the subsequent early texts: notably, a speech in which
Gertrude agrees to conceal and assist any stratagem of Hamlet's
against the King, and a related exchange in which Horatio reports
to the Queen (to her joy) the failure of Claudius' scheme to have
the Prince killed in England. Sometimes Q1 helps to resolve a
disputed reading, and occasionally its stage-directions are sharply
evocative. An example of the latter appears when Hamlet is
admonishing the Queen: '*Enter the ghost in his night gowne*'. [4]

The Second Quarto (Q2) was printed in 1604 and 1605. This
version is very long: at 3,723 lines, the longest of Shakespeare's
plays, approaching double the length of *Macbeth*. In general, the
quality of the speeches is superior to that in Q1, and the material is
thought to derive from Shakespeare's 'foul papers'; in other words,
from an untidy but authentic manuscript. Such stage-directions as

'*Enter old Polonius, with his man or two*' have a vagueness which indicate that the author was composing quite rapidly and had not worked out all the details. Q2 contains many small textual corruptions where the compositors had difficulty in reading Shakespeare's writing or were simply careless; and sometimes they printed words or phrases which the author had intended to delete. The manuscript may not have come in unrevised form: a play-house book-keeper may have emended it; and the printers then imposed (in varying degrees) their own conventions of layout, spelling and punctuation. Furthermore, they consulted a copy of Q1 (particularly when working on Act 1), so that the 'foul' Q2 has been contaminated by the 'bad' Q1. While the sheets of Q2 were being printed, a 'corrector' made small changes – some of which were fresh errors. Finally, although Q2 is so long, it still lacks two interesting passages, one describing Denmark as a prison (2.2.234–64 in the present text), the other dealing with the popularity of the boy actors (2.2.328–51).

You might expect that the First Folio would provide the best version of *Hamlet*, as that Folio volume was prepared by two of Shakespeare's fellow-actors, John Heminge (or Heminges) and Henry Condell, ostensibly as a memorial tribute to their colleague who had died in 1616. Certainly F1 contains about seventy lines not found in Q2, and its stage-directions (e.g. '*In scuffling they change Rapiers*') provide some useful clarifications. In various lines, the metre and phrasing have been improved. The snags, however, are these. First, F1 lacks 230 lines that were present in Q2. Secondly, some of the small additions in F1 may be actors' interpolations. Thirdly, F1 has a variety of new corruptions, many deriving from its team of compositors and particularly from the hapless compositor known to posterity only as 'B'.

Thus, anyone entrusted with the task of assembling a new edition of the play has a wide variety of options. Some editors give priority to Q2; some prefer F1; but usually they still have to use material from the other early texts. In the vast majority of cases, a conflated text emerges; but each editor's combination may differ significantly from that available elsewhere. Different editions offer different *Hamlet*s. Through all changes, an identity remains: *Hamlet* won't turn into a comedy or a cookery-book; but the critics will repeatedly be interpreting data which have already been manipulated, tidied, rearranged and rephrased in the light of the editors' critical assumptions. From a moral or psychoanalytical viewpoint, one of the most important speeches in the play is Hamlet's long soliloquy beginning 'How all occasions do inform against me'; but you won't find that speech in the body of the play edited by G. R. Hibbard (1987) or by Stanley Wells and Gary Taylor (1988). Those editors gave priority to the F1 version and relegated the Q2 additions to an Appendix.

In this edition, I have combined, as I think best, material from Q1, Q2 and F1. I have accepted various emendations offered by previous editors; and, as usual, the spellings and punctuation have often been modernised. The end-notes draw attention to particular textual problems and options. If you wish to gain a vivid sense of the differences between Q1, Q2 and F1, consult *The Three-Text Hamlet*. This big volume puts side-by-side, in columns, those early versions, so that you can see at a glance many of the discrepancies.

In short, there is more 'play' – flexibility, variability and adaptability – in *Hamlet* than you might at first imagine. The opportunities for readers, critics, actors and directors are admirably numerous. One reason for Shakespeare's durability is that the divergences, ambiguities and puzzles in the early texts provide plenty of room for later variations, adaptations and interpretations. In Shakespeare's day, the script of this tragedy was evidently changing in response to diverse needs and pressures; and, ever since, it has repeatedly been transformed in the imaginations of readers and audiences.

I hope that the present edition of *Hamlet* represents a useful compromise between the early texts, Shakespeare's intentions (insofar as they can be reasonably inferred) and modern requirements. The glossary explains unfamiliar terms, and the annotations offer clarification of obscurities. In any case, as you read the play, you may find that you are editing it to suit yourself, even as you are staging it in the boundless theatre of your imagination.

NOTES TO THIS SECTION:

1 Here and later, the line-totals are those specified by Harold Jenkins in his edition of *Hamlet* (London and New York: Methuen, 1982). These refer to the lines as printed, discounting stage-directions. Kathleen O. Irace, in her Introduction to *The First Quarto of Hamlet* (Cambridge: Cambridge University Press, 1998), p. 2, gives the line-totals as 2,221 (Q1), 4,056 (Q2) and 3,907 (F1).

2 Kathleen O. Irace found that 'a computer-assisted analysis . . . provided strong evidence confirming the hypothesis [of memorial reconstruction]'. See *The First Quarto of Hamlet*, pp. 6–7.

3 Q1 preserves lines corresponding to two passages which appear in F1 but not in Q2. These passages concern the 'war of the theatres' and Hamlet's regretting his treatment of Laertes.

4 Q1 and Q2 lack Act and scene divisions; F1 has a few near the beginning of the play.

NOTES ON THE SECTION

THE TRAGEDY OF HAMLET,
PRINCE OF DENMARK

CHARACTERS IN THE PLAY

CLAUDIUS, *King of Denmark*.

GERTRUDE, *Queen of Denmark, Hamlet's mother*.

HAMLET, *Prince of Denmark*.

HORATIO, *Hamlet's friend*.

POLONIUS, *the King's advisor*.

OPHELIA, *Polonius's daughter*.

LAERTES, *Polonius's son*.

REYNALDO, *Polonius's servant*.

VOLTEMAND *and* CORNELIUS, *Envoys*.

ROSENCRANTZ *and* GUILDERNSTERN.

OSRIC, *a courtier*.

MARCELLUS, BARNARDO *and* FRANCISCO, *sentinels*.

FORTINBRAS, *Prince of Norway*.

NORWEGIAN CAPTAIN.

SEVERAL PLAYERS.

TWO CLOWNS *(a grave-digger and his companion)*.

TWO ENGLISH AMBASSADORS.

SAILORS.

LORDS, COURTIERS, ATTENDANTS *and* SERVANTS.

GUARDS, SOLDIERS *and* MUSICIANS.

MESSENGER.

GHOST.

THE TRAGEDY OF HAMLET,
PRINCE OF DENMARK.

ACT I, SCENE I.

The castle at Elsinore. A platform upon the battlements.

Enter FRANCISCO, *a sentinel on guard. Enter* BARNARDO.

BARNARDO   Who's there?

FRANCISCO   Nay, answer *me*. Stand and unfold yourself.

BARNARDO   Long live the King!

FRANCISCO   Barnardo?

BARNARDO   He.

FRANCISCO   You come most carefully upon your hour.

BARNARDO   'Tis now struck twelve. Get thee to bed, Francisco.

FRANCISCO   For this relief much thanks. 'Tis bitter cold,
And I am sick at heart.

BARNARDO   Have you had quiet guard?

FRANCISCO   Not a mouse stirring.   10

BARNARDO   Well, good night.
If you do meet Horatio and Marcellus,
The rivals of my watch, bid them make haste.

Enter HORATIO *and* MARCELLUS.

FRANCISCO   I think I hear them. – Stand ho, who is there?

HORATIO   Friends to this ground.

MARCEL.   And liegemen to the Dane.[1]

FRANCISCO   Give you good night.

MARCEL.   O, farewell honest soldier;
Who hath relieved you?

FRANCISCO   Barnardo hath my place;
Give you good night.   [*Exit Francisco.*

MARCEL.   Holla, Barnardo!

BARNARDO   Say,
What, is Horatio there?

HORATIO   A piece of him.

BARNARDO   Welcome Horatio. Welcome, good Marcellus.   20

HORATIO	What, has this thing appeared again tonight?
BARNARDO	I have seen nothing.
MARCEL.	Horatio says 'tis but our fantasy,
	And will not let belief take hold of him
	Touching this dreaded sight twice seen of us.
	Therefore I have entreated him along
	With us to watch the minutes of this night,
	That if again this apparition come,
	He may approve our eyes and speak to it.
HORATIO	Tush, tush, 'twill not appear.
BARNARDO	Sit down awhile, 30
	And let us once again assail your ears,
	That are so fortified against our story,
	What we have two nights seen.
HORATIO	Well, sit we down,
	And let us hear Barnardo speak of this.
BARNARDO	Last night of all,
	When yon same star that's westward from the Pole
	Had made his course t'illume that part of heaven
	Where now it burns, Marcellus and myself,
	The bell then beating one –

Enter GHOST *in armour.*

MARCEL.	Peace, break thee off: look where it comes again! 40
BARNARDO	In the same figure like the King that's dead.
MARCEL.	Thou art a scholar, speak to it, Horatio.
BARNARDO	Looks a not like the King? Mark it, Horatio.
HORATIO	Most like; it harrows me with fear and wonder.
BARNARDO	It would be spoke to.
MARCEL.	Question it, Horatio.
HORATIO	What art thou that usurp'st this time of night,
	Together with that fair and warlike form
	In which the majesty of buried Denmark
	Did sometimes march? By heaven, I charge thee
	speak!
MARCEL.	It is offended.
BARNARDO	See, it stalks away. 50
HORATIO	Stay, speak, speak: I charge thee speak!

[*Exit Ghost.*

MARCEL.	'Tis gone and will not answer.
BARNARDO	How now, Horatio? You tremble and look pale.
	Is not this something more than fantasy?
	What think you on't?
HORATIO	Before my God, I might not this believe
	Without the sensible and true avouch
	Of mine own eyes.
MARCEL.	Is it not like the King?
HORATIO	As thou art to thyself.

Such was the very armour he had on,   60
When he the ambitious Norway combated.
So frowned he once, when in an angry parle
He smote the sledded Polacks[2] on the ice.
'Tis strange.

MARCEL.   Thus twice before, and jump at this dead hour,
With martial stalk hath he gone by our watch.

HORATIO   In what particular thought to work I know not,
But, in the gross and scope of mine opinion,
This bodes some strange eruption to our state.[3]

MARCEL.   Good now, sit down, and tell me he that knows,   70
Why this same strict and most observant watch
So nightly toils the subject of the land;
And why such daily cast of brazen cannon
And foreign mart for implements of war;
Why such impress of shipwrights, whose sore task
Does not divide the Sunday from the week?
What might be tóward that this sweaty haste
Doth make the night joint-labourer with the day?
Who is't that can inform me?

HORATIO   That can I —
At least the whisper goes so: our last King,   80
Whose image even but now appeared to us,
Was (as you know) by Fortinbras of Norway,
Thereto pricked on by a most emulate pride,
Dared to the combat; in which our valiant Hamlet
(For so this side of our known world esteemed him)
Did slay this Fortinbras, who by a sealed compáct,
Well ratified by law and heraldry,
Did forfeit (with his life) all those his lands

Which he stood seized of, to the conqueror,
Against the which a moiety competent   90
Was gagèd by our King, which had returned
To the inheritance of Fortinbras,
Had he been vanquisher; as, by the same cov'nant,[4]
And carriage of the article designed,
His fell to Hamlet. Now sir, young Fortinbras,
Of unimprovèd mettle hot and full,
Hath in the skirts of Norway here and there
Sharked up a list of lawless resolutes
For food and diet to some enterprise
That hath a stomach in't, which is no other   100
(As it doth well appear unto our state)
But to recover of us by strong hand
And terms compulsatory those foresaid lands
So by his father lost. And this (I take it)
Is the main motive of our preparations,
The source of this our watch, and the chief head
Of this post-haste and rummage in the land.

BARNARDO   I think it be no other but e'en so;
Well may it sort that this portentous figure
Comes armèd through our watch so like the King   110
That was and is the question of these wars.

HORATIO   A mote it is to trouble the mind's eye.
In the most high and palmy state of Rome,
A little ere the mightiest Julius fell,
The graves stood tenantless, and the sheeted dead
Did squeak and gibber in the Roman streets;[5]
Asters with trains of fire shed dews of blood,
Disastering the sun;[6] and the moist star,
Upon whose influence Neptune's empire stands,
Was sick almost to doomsday with eclipse.   120
And even the like precurse of fierce events,
As harbingers preceding still the fates
And prologue to the omen coming on,
Have heaven and earth together demonstrated
Unto our climatures and countrymen.[7]

Enter GHOST.

But soft, behold, lo where it comes again!

I'll cross it though it blast me.   [*He spreads his arms.*[8]

                              Stay, illusion:
If thou hast any sound or use of voice,
Speak to me.
If there be any good thing to be done   130
That may to thee do ease, and grace to me,
Speak to me.
If thou art privy to thy country's fate,
Which happily foreknowing may avoid,
O speak.
Or if thou hast uphoarded in thy life
Extorted treasure in the womb of earth,
For which they say you spirits oft walk in death,
                                   [*The cock crows.*
Speak of it – stay and speak! Stop it, Marcellus!

MARCEL.   Shall I strike at it with my partisan?   140

HORATIO   Do if it will not stand.

BARNARDO   'Tis here!

HORATIO   'Tis here! [*Exit Ghost.*

MARCEL.   'Tis gone!
We do it wrong, being so majestical,
To offer it the show of violence,
For it is as the air, invulnerable,
And our vain blows malicious mockery.

BARNARDO   It was about to speak when the cock crew.

HORATIO   And then it started like a guilty thing
Upon a fearful summons. I have heard,
The cock that is the trumpet to the morn   150
Doth with his lofty and shrill-sounding throat
Awake the god of day, and, at his warning,
Whether in sea or fire, in earth or air,
Th'extravagant and erring spirit hies
To his confine; and of the truth herein
This present object made probation.

MARCEL.   It faded on the crowing of the cock.
Some say that ever 'gainst that season comes
Wherein our Saviour's birth is celebrated,
This bird of dawning singeth all night long;   160
And then (they say) no spirit dare stir abroad,

The nights are wholesome, then no planets strike,
No fairy takes, nor witch hath power to charm,
So hallowed and so gracious is that time.

HORATIO   So have I heard, and do in part believe it.
But look, the morn in russet mantle clad
Walks o'er the dew of yon high eastward hill.
Break we our watch up, and by my advice
Let us impart what we have seen tonight
Unto young Hamlet; for upon my life   170
This spirit, dumb to us, will speak to him.
Do you consent we shall acquaint him with it,
As needful in our loves, fitting our duty?

MARCEL.   Let's do't, I pray, and I this morning know
Where we shall find him most convenient.

                                                [Exeunt.

SCENE 2.

The Council Chamber in the castle.

A flourish of trumpets. Enter CLAUDIUS, *King of Denmark,*
GERTRUDE *the Queen, Prince* HAMLET *(dressed in black),*
and COUNCILLORS *including* POLONIUS *and his son* LAERTES,
VOLTEMAND *and* CORNELIUS.

KING   Though yet of Hamlet our dear brother's death
The memory be green, and that it us befitted
To bear our hearts in grief, and our whole kingdom
To be contracted in one brow of woe,
Yet so far hath discretion fought with nature,
That we with wisest sorrow think on him
Together with remembrance of ourselves.
Therefore our sometime sister, now our Queen,
Th'imperial jointress to this warlike state,
Have we, as 'twere with a defeated joy,   10
With an auspicious and a dropping eye,
With mirth in funeral, and with dirge in marriage,
In equal scale weighing delight and dole,
Taken to wife. Nor have we herein barred

Your better wisdoms, which have freely gone
With this affair along: for all, our thanks.
Now follows that you know: young Fortinbras,
Holding a weak supposal of our worth,
Or thinking by our late dear brother's death
Our state to be disjoint and out of frame,   20
Colleaguèd with this dream of his advantage –
He hath not failed to pester us with message
Importing the surrender of those lands
Lost by his father, with all bonds of law,
To our most valiant brother. So much for him.
Now for ourself, and for this time of meeting,
Thus much the business is. We have here writ
To Norway, uncle of young Fortinbras –
Who, impotent and bed-rid, scarcely hears
Of this his nephew's purpose – to suppress   30
His further gait herein, in that the levies,
The lists and full proportions are all made
Out of his subject; and we here dispatch
You, good Cornelius, and you, Voltemand,
For bearers of this greeting to old Norway,
Giving to you no further personal power
To business with the King, more than the scope
Of these dilated articles allow.
Farewell, and let your haste commend your duty.

CORNEL., VOLTEM.   In that, and all things, will we show our duty. 40

KING   We doubt it nothing; heartily farewell.

                              [*Exeunt Voltemand and Cornelius.*

And now, Laertes, what's the news with you?
You told us of some suit: what is't, Laertes?
You cannot speak of reason to the Dane
And lose your voice. What wouldst thou beg, Laertes,
That shall not be my offer, not thy asking?
The head is not more native to the heart,
The hand more instrumental to the mouth,
Than is the throne of Denmark to thy father.
What wouldst thou have, Laertes?

LAERTES   My dread lord,   50
Your leave and favour to return to France,

From whence though willingly I came to Denmark
To show my duty in your coronation,
Yet now I must confess, that duty done,
My thoughts and wishes bend again toward France,
And bow them to your gracious leave and pardon.

KING   Have you your father's leave? What says Polonius?

POLONIUS   He hath, my lord, wrung from me my slow leave
By laboursome petition, and at last
Upon his will I sealed my hard consent.   60
I do beseech you give him leave to go.

KING   Take thy fair hour, Laertes, time be thine,
And thy best graces spend it at thy will.
But now, my cousin Hamlet, and my son –

HAMLET   A little more than kin, and less than kind.[9]

KING   How is it that the clouds still hang on you?

HAMLET   Not so, my lord, I am too much in the sun.[10]

QUEEN   Good Hamlet, cast thy nighted colour off,
And let thine eye look like a friend on Denmark.
Do not for ever with thy vailed lids   70
Seek for thy noble father in the dust.
Thou know'st 'tis common, all that lives must die,
Passing through nature to eternity.

HAMLET   Ay, madam, it is common.

QUEEN   If it be,
Why seems it so particular with thee?

HAMLET   'Seems', madam? Nay, it *is*; I know not 'seems'.
'Tis not alone my inky cloak, good mother,
Nor customary suits of solemn black,
Nor windy suspiration of forced breath,
No, nor the fruitful river in the eye,   80
Nor the dejected haviour of the visage,
Together with all forms, moods, shows of grief,
That can denote me truly. These indeed seem,
For they are actions that a man might play;
But I have that within which passes show;
These, but the trappings and the suits of woe.

KING   'Tis sweet and commendable in your nature, Hamlet,
To give these mourning duties to your father;
But you must know, your father lost a father;

That father lost, lost his; and the survivor bound   90
In filial obligation for some term
To do obsequious sorrow. But to perséver
In obstinate condolement is a course
Of impious stubbornness. 'Tis unmanly grief:
It shows a will most incorrect to heaven,
A heart unfortified, a mind impatient,
An understanding simple and unschooled.
For, what we know must be, and is as common
As any the most vulgar thing to sense,
Why should we in our peevish opposition   100
Take it to heart? Fie, 'tis a fault to heaven,
A fault against the dead, a fault to nature,
To reason most absurd, whose common theme
Is death of fathers, and who still hath cried,
From the first corse till he that died today,
'This must be so'. We pray you throw to earth
This unprevailing woe, and think of us
As of a father; for let the world take note,
You are the most immediate to our throne,
And with no less nobility of love   110
Than that which dearest father bears his son
Do I impart toward you. For your intent
In going back to school in Wittenberg,
It is most retrograde to our desire,
And we beseech you, bend you to remain
Here in the cheer and comfort of our eye,
Our chiefest courtier, cousin, and our son.

QUEEN   Let not thy mother lose her prayers, Hamlet;
I pray thee stay with us, go not to Wittenberg.

HAMLET   I shall in all my best obey you, madam.   120

KING   Why, 'tis a loving and a fair reply.
Be as ourself in Denmark. Madam, come.
This gentle and unforced accord of Hamlet
Sits smiling to my heart; in grace whereof,
No jocund health that Denmark drinks today,
But the great cannon to the clouds shall tell,
And the King's rouse the heaven shall bruit again,
Re-speaking earthly thunder. Come away.

[Flourish. Exeunt all but Hamlet.

HAMLET   O, that this too too solid flesh[11] would melt,
          Thaw and resolve itself into a dew,   130
          Or that the Everlasting had not fixed
          His canon 'gainst self-slaughter.[12] O God, God,
          How weary, stale, flat and unprofitable
          Seem to me all the uses of this world!
          Fie on't, ah fie, 'tis an unweeded garden
          That grows to seed; things rank and gross in nature
          Possess it merely. That it should come to this!
          But two months dead – nay not so much, not two –
          So excellent a king, that was to this
          Hyperion to a satyr; so loving to my mother,   140
          That he might not beteem the winds of heaven
          Visit her face too roughly. Heaven and earth,
          Must I remember? Why, she would hang on him
          As if increase of appetite had grown
          By what it fed on, and yet within a month –
          Let me not think on't: frailty, thy name is woman –
          A little month, or ere those shoes were old
          With which she followed my poor father's body,
          Like Niobe all tears, why she, even she –
          O God, a beast that wants discourse of reason   150
          Would have mourned longer – married with my uncle,
          My father's brother, but no more like my father
          Than I to Hercules; within a month,
          Ere yet the salt of most unrighteous tears
          Had left the flushing in her gallèd eyes,
          She married. O most wicked speed, to post
          With such dexterity to incestuous sheets![13]
          It is not (nor it cannot come to) good.
          But break, my heart, for I must hold my tongue.

          Enter HORATIO, MARCELLUS *and* BARNARDO.

HORATIO   Hail to your lordship!
HAMLET   I am glad to see you well.   160
          Horatio – or I do forget myself!
HORATIO   The same, my lord, and your poor servant ever.
HAMLET   Sir, my good friend, I'll change that name with you.

	And what make you from Wittenberg, Horatio? – Marcellus.	
MARCEL.	My good lord.	
HAMLET	I am very glad to see you. [*To Barnardo:*] Good even, sir. – But what in faith make you from Wittenberg?	
HORATIO	A truant disposition, good my lord.	
HAMLET	I would not hear your enemy say so, Nor shall you do mine ear that violence To make it truster of your own report Against yourself. I know you are no truant. But what is your affair in Elsinore? We'll teach you to drink deep ere you depart.	170
HORATIO	My lord, I came to see your father's funeral.	
HAMLET	I prithee do not mock me, fellow-student; I think it was to see my mother's wedding.	
HORATIO	Indeed, my lord, it followed hard upon.	
HAMLET	Thrift, thrift, Horatio: the funeral baked meats Did coldly furnish forth the marriage tables. Would I had met my dearest foe in heaven Ere I had ever seen that day, Horatio. My father – methinks I see my father –	180
HORATIO	Where, my lord?	
HAMLET	In my mind's eye, Horatio.	
HORATIO	I saw him once. He was a goodly king –	
HAMLET	He was a man, take him for all in all: I shall not look upon his like again.	
HORATIO	My lord, I think I saw him yesternight.	
HAMLET	Saw, who?	190
HORATIO	My lord, the King your father.	
HAMLET	The King my father!	
HORATIO	Season your admiration for a while With an attent ear, till I may deliver, Upon the witness of these gentlemen, This marvel to you.	
HAMLET	For God's love let me hear!	
HORATIO	Two nights together had these gentlemen, Marcellus and Barnardo, on their watch In the dead waste and middle of the night, Been thus encountered. A figure like your father,	

Armed at all points exactly, cap-à-pie,   200
Appears before them, and with solemn march
Goes slow and stately by them; thrice he walked
By their oppressed and fear-surprisèd eyes
Within his truncheon's length, whilst they, distilled
Almost to jelly with the act of fear,
Stand dumb and speak not to him. This to me
In dreadful secrecy impart they did,
And I with them the third night kept the watch,
Where, as they had delivered, both in time,
Form of the thing, each word made true and good,   210
The apparition comes. I knew your father;
These hands are not more like.

HAMLET	But where was this?
MARCEL.	My lord, upon the platform where we watch.
HAMLET	Did you not speak to it?
HORATIO	My lord, I did,

But answer made it none. Yet once methought
It lifted up its head, and did address
Itself to motion like as it would speak;
But even then the morning cock crew loud,
And at the sound it shrunk in haste away
And vanished from our sight.

HAMLET	'Tis very strange. 220
HORATIO	As I do live, my honoured lord, 'tis true;

And we did think it writ down in our duty
To let you know of it.

HAMLET	Indeed, indeed, sirs, but this troubles me.
	Hold you the watch tonight?
ALL	We do, my lord.
HAMLET	Armed, say you?
ALL	Armed, my lord.
HAMLET	From top to toe?
ALL	My lord, from head to foot.
HAMLET	Then saw you not his face.
HORATIO	O yes, my lord, he wore his beaver up.
HAMLET	What, looked he frowningly?
HORATIO	A countenance more in sorrow than in anger. 230
HAMLET	Pale, or red?

HORATIO	Nay, very pale.
HAMLET	And fixed his eyes upon you?
HORATIO	Most constantly.
HAMLET	I would I had been there.
HORATIO	It would have much amazed you.
HAMLET	Very like, very like. Stayed it long?
HORATIO	While one with moderate haste might tell a hundred.
MARCEL., BARN.	Longer, longer.
HORATIO	Not when I saw't.
HAMLET	His beard was grizzled, no?
HORATIO	It was, as I have seen it in his life, A sable silvered.
HAMLET	I will watch tonight: Perchance 'twill walk again.
HORATIO	I war'nt it will.
HAMLET	If it assume my noble father's person, I'll speak to it though hell itself should gape And bid me hold my peace. I pray you all, If you have hitherto concealed this sight, Let it be tenable in your silence still; And whatsoever else shall hap tonight, Give it an understanding but no tongue. I will requite your loves; so, fare you well: Upon the platform 'twixt eleven and twelve I'll visit you.
ALL	Our duty to your honour.
HAMLET	Your loves, as mine to you. Farewell.

240

250

[*Exeunt.*

My father's spirit in arms? All is not well;
I doubt some foul play. Would the night were come.
Till then, sit still my soul; foul deeds will rise,
Though all the earth o'erwhelm them, to men's eyes.

[*Exit.*

SCENE 3.

Enter LAERTES *and* OPHELIA.

LAERTES My necessaries are embarked. Farewell.
And sister, as the winds give benefit
And convoy is assistant, do not sleep,
But let me hear from you.

OPHELIA   Do you doubt that?

LAERTES For Hamlet, and the trifling of his favour,
Hold it a fashion and a toy in blood,
A violet in the youth of primy nature,
Forward, not permanent, sweet, not lasting,
The perfume and suppliance of a minute,
No more.

OPHELIA   No more but so?

LAERTES   Think it no more.   10
For nature crescent does not grow alone
In thews and bulk, but, as this temple waxes,
The inward service of the mind and soul
Grows wide withal. Perhaps he loves you now,
And now no soil nor cautel doth besmirch
The virtue of his will; but you must fear,
His greatness weighed, his will is not his own,
For he himself is subject to his birth.
He may not, as unvalued persons do,
Carve for himself, for on his choice depends   20
The sanity and health of this whole state;
And therefore must his choice be circumscribed
Unto the voice and yielding of that body
Whereof he is the head. Then if he says he loves you,
It fits your wisdom so far to believe it
As he in his particular act and place
May give his saying deed, which is no further
Than the main voice of Denmark goes withal.
Then weigh what loss your honour may sustain
If with too credent ear you list his songs,   30
Or lose your heart, or your chaste treasure open

        To his unmastered importunity.
        Fear it, Ophelia, fear it, my dear sister,
        And keep you in the rear of your affection,
        Out of the shot and danger of desire.
        The chariest maid is prodigal enough
        If she unmask her beauty to the moon.[14]
        Virtue itself scapes not calumnious strokes.
        The canker galls the infants of the spring
        Too oft before their buttons be disclosed,   40
        And in the morn and liquid dew of youth
        Contagious blastments are most imminent.
        Be wary then: best safety lies in fear;
        Youth to itself rebels, though none else near.[15]

OPHELIA   I shall the effect of this good lesson keep
        As watchman to my heart. But good my brother,
        Do not, as some ungracious pastors do,
        Show me the steep and thorny way to heaven,
        Whilst, like a puffed and reckless libertine,
        Himself the primrose path of dalliance treads,   50
        And recks not his own rede.

                Enter POLONIUS.

LAERTES   O fear me not.
        I stay too long – but here my father comes.
        A double blessing is a double grace;
        Occasion smiles upon a second leave.

POLONIUS   Yet here, Laertes? Aboard, aboard for shame!
        The wind sits in the shoulder of your sail,
        And you are stayed for. There – my blessing with thee,
        And these few precepts in thy memory
        See thou charácter. Give thy thoughts no tongue,
        Nor any unproportioned thought his act.   60
        Be thou familiar, but by no means vulgar;
        Those friends thou hast, and their adoption tried,
        Grapple them to thy soul with hoops of steel,
        But do not dull thy palm with entertainment
        Of each new-hatched unfledged comrade.[16] Beware
        Of entrance to a quarrel, but being in,
        Bear't that th'opposèd may beware of thee.

Give every man thy ear, but few thy voice;
Take each man's censure, but reserve thy judgement.
Costly thy habit as thy purse can buy, 70
But not expressed in fancy; rich, not gaudy;
For the apparel oft proclaims the man,
And they in France of the best rank and station
Are most select and generous, chief in that.[17]
Neither a borrower nor a lender be,
For loan oft loses both itself and friend,
And borrowing dulls the edge of husbandry.
This above all: to thine own self be true;
And it must follow, as the night the day,
Thou canst not then be false to any man. 80
Farewell; my blessing season this in thee.

LAERTES   Most humbly do I take my leave, my lord.

POLONIUS   The time invites you: go, your servants tend.

LAERTES   Farewell, Ophelia, and remember well
What I have said to you.

OPHELIA   'Tis in my memory locked,
And you yourself shall keep the key of it.

LAERTES   Farewell.   [Exit.

POLONIUS   What is't, Ophelia, he hath said to you?

OPHELIA   So please you, something touching the Lord Hamlet.

POLONIUS   Marry, well bethought. 90
'Tis told me he hath very oft of late
Given private time to you, and you yourself
Have of your audience been most free and bounteous.
If it be so — as so 'tis put on me,
And that in way of caution — I must tell you,
You do not understand yourself so clearly
As it behoves my daughter and your honour.
What is between you? Give me up the truth.

OPHELIA   He hath, my lord, of late made many tenders
Of his affection to me. 100

POLONIUS   Affection, pooh! You speak like a green girl
Unsifted in such perilous circumstance.
Do you believe his 'tenders', as you call them?

OPHELIA   I do not know, my lord, what I should think.

POLONIUS   Marry, I will teach you. Think yourself a baby,

That you have ta'en these tenders for true pay
Which are not sterling. Tender yourself more dearly,
Or (not to crack the wind of the poor phrase,
Running it thus)[18] you'll tender me a fool.

OPHELIA   My lord, he hath impórtuned me with love   110
In honourable fashion —

POLONIUS   Ay, 'fashion' you may call it; go to, go to.

OPHELIA   And hath given countenance to his speech, my lord,
With almost all the holy vows of heaven.

POLONIUS   Ay, springes to catch woodcocks. I do know,
When the blood burns, how prodigal the soul
Lends the tongue vows. These blazes, daughter,
Giving more light than heat, extinct in both
Even in their promise as it is a-making,
You must not take for fire. From this time[19]   120
Be something scanter of your maiden presence;
Set your entreatments at a higher rate
Than a command to parley. For Lord Hamlet,
Believe so much in him: that he is young,
And with a larger tether may he walk
Than may be given you. In few, Ophelia,
Do not believe his vows, for they are brokers
Not of that dye which their investments show,
But mere implorators of unholy suits,
Breathing like sanctified and pious bonds[20]   130
The better to beguile. This is for all.
I would not — in plain terms — from this time forth
Have you so slander any moment leisure
As to give words or talk with the Lord Hamlet.
Look to't, I charge you; come your ways.

OPHELIA   I shall obey, my lord.

                                            [*Exeunt.*

SCENE 4.

The platform on the battlements.

Enter HAMLET, HORATIO *and* MARCELLUS.

HAMLET	The air bites shrewdly; it is very cold.
HORATIO	It is a nipping and an eager air.
HAMLET	What hour now?
HORATIO	I think it lacks of twelve.
MARCEL.	No, it is struck.
HORATIO	Indeed? I heard it not.

HORATIO   It then draws near the season
Wherein the spirit held his wont to walk.
    [*Offstage, a flourish of trumpets, and two cannon are fired.*
What does this mean, my lord?

HAMLET   The King doth wake tonight and takes his rouse,
Keeps wassail and the swagg'ring upspring reels;[21]
And, as he drains his draughts of Rhenish down,   10
The kettle-drum and trumpet thus bray out
The triumph of his pledge.

HORATIO   Is it a custom?

HAMLET   Ay marry is't;
But to my mind, though I am native here
And to the manner born, it is a custom
More honoured in the breach than the observance.[22]
This heavy-headed revel east and west
Makes us traduced and taxed of other nations.
They clepe us drunkards, and with swinish phrase
Soil our addition; and indeed it takes   20
From our achievements, though performed at height,
The pith and marrow of our attribute.
So, oft it chances in particular men,
That for some vicious mole of nature in them,
As in their birth, wherein they are not guilty
(Since nature cannot choose his origin),
By the o'ergrowth of some complexion,
Oft breaking down the pales and forts of reason,
Or by some habit, that too much o'er-leavens

The form of plausive manners – that these men,   30
Carrying, I say, the stamp of one defect,
Being Nature's livery, or Fortune's star,
His virtues else, be they as pure as grace,
As infinite as man may undergo,
Shall in the general censure take corruption
From that particular fault. The dram of evil
Doth all the noble substance of a doubt,
To his own scandal.[23]

Enter GHOST.

HORATIO   Look, my lord, it comes!
HAMLET   Angels and ministers of grace defend us!
Be thou a spirit of health, or goblin damned,   40
Bring with thee airs from heaven, or blasts from hell,
Be thy intents wicked, or charitable,
Thou com'st in such a questionable shape
That I will speak to thee. I'll call thee Hamlet,
King, father, royal Dane. O, answer me!
Let me not rest in ignorance,[24] but tell
Why thy canónized bones, hearsèd in death,
Have burst their cerements; why the sepulchre,
Wherein we saw thee quietly interred,[25]
Hath oped his ponderous and marble jaws   50
To cast thee up again. What may this mean
That thou, dead corse, again in cómplete steel,
Revisits thus the glimpses of the moon,
Making night hideous, and we fools of nature
So horridly to shake our disposition
With thoughts beyond the reaches of our souls?
Say, why is this? Wherefore? What should we do?
                    [*Ghost beckons Hamlet.*

HORATIO   It beckons you to go away with it,
As if it some impartment did desire
To you alone.
MARCEL.   Look with what courteous action   60
It waves you to a more removèd ground.
But do not go with it.
HORATIO   No, by no means.

HAMLET   It will not speak. Then I will follow it.
HORATIO   Do not, my lord.
HAMLET   Why, what should be the fear?
          I do not set my life at a pin's fee,
          And for my soul, what can it do to that,
          Being a thing immortal as itself?
          It waves me forth again. I'll follow it.
HORATIO   What if it tempt you toward the flood, my lord,
          Or to the dreadful summit of the cliff   70
          That beetles o'er his base into the sea,
          And there assume some other horrible form,
          Which might deprive your sovereignty of reason,
          And draw you into madness? Think of it –
          The very place puts toys of desperation,
          Without more motive, into every brain
          That looks so many fathoms to the sea
          And hears it roar beneath.[26]
HAMLET   It waves me still.
          – Go on, I'll follow thee.
MARCEL.   You shall not go, my lord.
HAMLET   Hold off your hands.   80
HORATIO   Be ruled, you shall not go.
HAMLET   My fate cries out,
          And makes each petty artere in this body
          As hardy as the Némean lion's nerve.
          Still am I called. Unhand me gentlemen.
                    [*He breaks from them, drawing his sword.*
          By heaven, I'll make a ghost of him that lets me!
          I say, away! – Go on, I'll follow thee.
                              [*Exit Ghost, Hamlet following.*
HORATIO   He waxes desperate with imagination.
MARCEL.   Let's follow: 'tis not fit thus to obey him.
HORATIO   Have after. To what issue will this come?
MARCEL.   Something is rotten in the state of Denmark.   90
HORATIO   Heaven will direct it.
MARCEL.   Nay, let's follow him.
                                                  [*Exeunt.*

SCENE 5.

Enter GHOST *and* HAMLET.

HAMLET   Whither wilt thou lead me? Speak, I'll go no further.

GHOST   Mark me.

HAMLET   I will.

GHOST   My hour is almost come,
When I to sulph'rous and tormenting flames
Must render up myself.

HAMLET   Alas, poor ghost!

GHOST   Pity me not, but lend thy serious hearing
To what I shall unfold.

HAMLET   Speak: I am bound to hear.

GHOST   So art thou to revenge, when thou shalt hear.

HAMLET   What?

GHOST   I am thy father's spirit,
Doomed for a certain term to walk the night,   10
And for the day confined to fast in fires[27]
Till the foul crimes done in my days of nature
Are burnt and purged away. But that I am forbid
To tell the secrets of my prison-house,
I could a tale unfold whose lightest word
Would harrow up thy soul, freeze thy young blood,
Make thy two eyes like stars start from their spheres,
Thy knotted and combinèd locks to part,
And each particular hair to stand on end,
Like quills upon the fretful porpentine.   20
But things eternal blazoned must not be[28]
To ears of flesh and blood. List, list, O list!
If thou didst ever thy dear father love —

HAMLET   O God!

GHOST   Revenge his foul and most unnatural murder.

HAMLET   Murder!

GHOST   Murder most foul, as in the best it is,
But this most foul, strange and unnatural.

HAMLET   Haste me to know't, that I with wings as swift
As meditation or the thoughts of love   30

May sweep to my revenge.

GHOST   I find thee apt,
And duller shouldst thou be than the fat weed
That rots itself in ease on Lethe wharf,[29]
Wouldst thou not stir in this. Now Hamlet, hear.
'Tis given out, that sleeping in my orchard,
A serpent stung me; so the whole ear of Denmark
Is by a forgèd process of my death
Rankly abused. But know, thou noble youth,
The serpent that did sting thy father's life
Now wears his crown.

HAMLET   O, my prophetic soul!   40
My uncle?

GHOST   Ay! That incestuous, that adulterate beast,
With witchcraft of his wit, with traitorous gifts –
O wicked wit and gifts, that have the power
So to seduce! – won to his shameful lust
The will of my most seeming-virtuous Queen.
O Hamlet, what a falling-off was there:
From me, whose love was of that dignity
That it went hand in hand even with the vow
I made to her in marriage; and to decline   50
Upon a wretch whose natural gifts were poor
To those of mine.
But virtue, as it never will be moved,
Though lewdness court it in a shape of heaven,
So lust, though to a radiant angel linked,
Will sate itself in a celestial bed
And prey on garbage.
But soft, methinks I scent the morning air:
Brief let me be. Sleeping within my orchard,
My custom always of the afternoon,   60
Upon my sécure hour thy uncle stole
With juice of cursed hebona in a vial,
And in the porches of my ears did pour[30]
The leperous distilment, whose effect
Holds such an enmity with blood of man
That swift as quicksilver it courses through
The natural gates and alleys of the body,

And with a sudden vigour it doth posset
And curd, like eager droppings into milk,
The thin and wholesome blood; so did it mine,   70
And a most instant tetter barked about
Most lazar-like with vile and loathsome crust
All my smooth body.
Thus was I, sleeping, by a brother's hand,
Of life, of crown, of Queen at once dispatched,
Cut off even in the blossoms of my sin,
Unhouseled, disappointed, unaneled,
No reck'ning made, but sent to my account
With all my imperfections on my head.
O horrible! O horrible! Most horrible !   80
If thou hast nature in thee, bear it not.
Let not the royal bed of Denmark be
A couch for luxury and damned incest.
But howsoever thou pursuest this act,
Taint not thy mind, nor let thy soul contrive
Against thy mother aught. Leave her to heaven,
And to those thorns that in her bosom lodge
To prick and sting her. Fare thee well at once.
The glow-worm shows the matin to be near,
And 'gins to pale his uneffectual fire.   90
Adieu, adieu, adieu. Remember me.

                              [Exit Ghost.

HAMLET   O all you host of heaven! O earth! What else?
And shall I couple hell? O fie! Hold, hold, my heart,
And you, my sinews, grow not instant old,
But bear me stiffly up. Remember thee?
Ay, thou poor ghost, while memory holds a seat
In this distracted globe. Remember thee?
Yea, from the table of my memory
I'll wipe away all trivial fond recórds,
All saws of books, all forms, all pressures past   100
That youth and observation copied there,
And thy commandment all alone shall live
Within the book and volume of my brain,
Unmixed with baser matter; yes, by heaven!
O most pernicious woman!

O villain, villain, smiling damnèd villain!
My tables: meet it is I set it down   [*He writes.*
That one may smile, and smile, and be a villain –
At least I'm sure it may be so in Denmark.
So, uncle, there you are. Now, to my word.   110
It is 'Adieu, adieu. Remember me.'
I have sworn't.

                    Enter HORATIO *and* MARCELLUS.

HORATIO	My lord, my lord!
HAMLET	Lord Hamlet!
HORATIO	Heaven secure him!
HAMLET	So be it.
MARCEL.	Hillo, ho, ho, my lord!
HAMLET	Hillo, ho, ho, boy! Come, bird, come.[31]
MARCEL.	How is't, my noble lord?
HORATIO	What news, my lord?
HAMLET	O, wonderful!
HORATIO	Good my lord, tell it.
HAMLET	No,

You will reveal it.

HORATIO	Not I, my lord, by heaven.
MARCEL.	Nor I, my lord. 120
HAMLET	How say you then, would heart of man once think it?
	But you'll be secret?
HORATIO, MARCEL.	Ay, by heaven, my lord.
HAMLET	There's ne'er a villain dwelling in all Denmark
	But he's an arrant knave.
HORATIO	There needs no ghost, my lord, come from the grave,
	To tell us this.
HAMLET	Why right, you are in the right,

And so without more circumstance at all
I hold it fit that we shake hands and part:
You, as your business and desire shall point you,
For every man hath business and desire,   130
Such as it is; and for my own poor part,
Look you, I will go pray.

HORATIO	These are but wild and whirling words, my lord.
HAMLET	I am sorry they offend you, heartily,

Yes, faith, heartily.

HORATIO   There's no offence, my lord.

HAMLET   [*to Horatio:*] Yes, by Saint Patrick,[32] but there is, Horatio,
And much offence too. Touching this vision here,
It is an honest ghost, that let me tell you.
For your desire to know what is between us,
O'ermaster't as you may.

                      [*To both:*] And now, good friends,   140
As you are friends, scholars, and soldiers,
Give me one poor request.

HORATIO   What is't, my lord? We will.

HAMLET   Never make known what you have seen tonight.

BOTH   My lord, we will not.

HAMLET   Nay, but swear't.

HORATIO   In faith,
My lord, not I.

MARCEL.   Nor I, my lord, in faith.

HAMLET   [*draws:*] Upon my sword.

MARCEL.   We have sworn, my lord, already.

HAMLET   Indeed, upon my sword, indeed.

GHOST   [*beneath:*] Swear.

HAMLET   Ah ha, boy! Say'st thou so? Art thou there, truepenny?
Come on, you hear this fellow in the cellarage: 150
Consent to swear.

HORATIO   Propose the oath, my lord.

HAMLET   Never to speak of this that you have seen:
Swear by my sword.

               [*They lay their hands upon the hilt.*

GHOST   [*beneath:*] Swear.   [*They swear.*[33]

HAMLET   *Hic et ubique?* Then we'll shift our ground.
Come hither, gentlemen,
And lay your hands again upon my sword.
Swear by my sword
Never to speak of this that you have heard.

GHOST   [*beneath:*] Swear by his sword.   [*They swear.*   160

HAMLET   Well said, old mole! Canst work i'th'earth so fast?
A worthy pioner! Once more remove, good friends.

HORATIO   O day and night, but this is wondrous strange!

HAMLET   And therefore as a stranger give it welcome.

There are more things in heaven and earth, Horatio,
Than are dreamt of in your philosophy.[34]
But come:
Here as before, never, so help you mercy,
How strange or odd soe'er I bear myself –
As I perchance hereafter shall think meet   170
To put an antic disposition on –
That you at such times seeing me, never shall
With arms encumbered thus, or this head-shake,
Or by pronouncing of some doubtful phrase,
As 'Well, well, we know', or 'We could an if we
                                                    would',
Or 'If we list to speak', or 'There be an if they might',
Or such ambiguous giving out, to note
That you know aught of me: this not to do,
So grace and mercy at your most need help you!
Swear.   180

GHOST   [beneath:] Swear.   [They swear.
HAMLET   Rest, rest, perturbèd spirit! – So, gentlemen,
With all my love I do commend me to you,
And what so poor a man as Hamlet is
May do t'express his love and friending to you,
God willing shall not lack. Let us go in together,
And still your fingers on your lips, I pray.
The time is out of joint: O cursèd spite,
That ever I was born to set it right!
Nay come, let's go together.   190
                                                    [Exeunt.

ACT 2, SCENE I.

Enter POLONIUS *and* REYNALDO.

POLONIUS Give him this money, and these notes, Reynaldo.
REYNALDO I will, my lord.
POLONIUS You shall do marvellous wisely, good Reynaldo,
          Before you visit him, to make inquire
          Of his behaviour.
REYNALDO   My lord, I did intend it.
POLONIUS Marry, well said, very well said. Look you, sir,
          Inquire me first what Danskers are in Paris,
          And how, and who, what means, and where they keep,
          What company, at what expense; and finding
          By this encompassment and drift of question   10
          That they do know my son, come you more nearer
          Than your particular demands will touch it.
          Take you as 'twere some distant knowledge of him,
          As thus, 'I know his father, and his friends,
          And in part him' – do you mark this, Reynaldo?
REYNALDO Ay, very well, my lord.
POLONIUS 'And in part him, but', you may say, 'not well,
          But if't be he I mean, he's very wild,
          Addicted so and so'; and there put on him
          What forgeries you please; marry, none so rank   20
          As may dishonour him – take heed of that –
          But, sir, such wanton, wild, and usual slips
          As are companions noted and most known
          To youth and liberty.
REYNALDO   As gaming, my lord.
POLONIUS Ay, or drinking, fencing, swearing,
          Quarrelling, drabbing – you may go so far.
REYNALDO My lord, that would dishonour him.
POLONIUS Faith no, as you may season it in the charge.[35]
          You must not put another scandal on him,
          That he is open to incontinency –   30
          That's not my meaning; but breathe his faults so quaintly
          That they may seem the taints of liberty,

The flash and outbreak of a fiery mind,
A savageness in unreclaimèd blood,
Of general assault.

REYNALDO   But, my good lord –
POLONIUS   Wherefore should you do this?
REYNALDO   Ay my lord,
I would know that.
POLONIUS   Marry sir, here's my drift,
And I believe it is a fetch of warrant.
You laying these slight sullies on my son,
As 'twere a thing a little soiled i'th' working,   40
Mark you, your party in converse, him you would
                                                           sound,
Having ever seen in the prenominate crimes
The youth you breathe of guilty, be assured
He closes with you in this consequence,
'Good sir', or so, or 'friend', or 'gentleman',
According to the phrase, or the addition
Of man and country.
REYNALDO   Very good, my lord.
POLONIUS   And then sir, does he this, he does – What was I about
to say? By the Mass, I was about to say something.
Where did I leave?
REYNALDO   At 'closes in the consequence',   50
At 'friend, or so', and 'gentleman'.
POLONIUS   At 'closes in the consequence'; ay marry:
He closes thus: 'I know the gentleman,
I saw him yesterday', or 'th'other day',
Or then, or then, with such or such; 'and as you say,
There was he gaming, there o'ertook in's rouse,
There falling out at tennis', or perchance,
'I saw him enter such a house of sale',
Videlicet, a brothel, or so forth. See you now,
Your bait of falsehood takes this carp of truth,   60
And thus do we of wisdom and of reach,
With windlasses and with assays of bias,
By indirections find directions out.
So by my former lecture and advice
Shall you my son; you have me, have you not?

REYNALDO   My lord, I have.

POLONIUS   God buy ye, fare ye well.

REYNALDO   Good my lord.

POLONIUS   Observe his inclination in yourself.

REYNALDO   I shall, my lord.

POLONIUS   And let him ply his music.

REYNALDO   Well, my lord.   [*Exit.*   70

POLONIUS   Farewell.

Enter OPHELIA.

                How now Ophelia, what's the matter?

OPHELIA   Alas, my lord, I have been so affrighted!

POLONIUS   With what, i'th'name of God?

OPHELIA   My lord, as I was sewing in my chamber,
Lord Hamlet, with his doublet all unbraced,
No hat upon his head, his stockings fouled,
Ungartered and down-gyvèd to his ankle,
Pale as his shirt, his knees knocking each other,
And with a look so piteous in purport
As if he had been loosèd out of hell   80
To speak of horrors – he comes before me.

POLONIUS   Mad for thy love?

OPHELIA   My lord, I do not know,
But truly I do fear it.

POLONIUS   What said he?

OPHELIA   He took me by the wrist, and held me hard,
Then goes he to the length of all his arm,
And, with his other hand thus o'er his brow,
He falls to such perusal of my face
As he would draw it. Long stayed he so.
At last, a little shaking of mine arm,
And thrice his head thus waving up and down,   90
He raised a sigh so piteous and profound
That it did seem to shatter all his bulk
And end his being. That done, he lets me go,
And with his head over his shoulder turned,
He seemed to find his way without his eyes,
For out adoors he went without their help;
And to the last bended their light on me.

POLONIUS   Come, go with me. I will go seek the King.
            This is the very ecstasy of love,
            Whose violent property fordoes itself   100
            And leads the will to desperate undertakings
            As oft as any passion under heaven
            That does afflict our natures. I am sorry –
            What, have you given him any hard words of late?

OPHELIA   No, my good lord, but, as you did command,
            I did repel his letters, and denied
            His access to me.

POLONIUS   That hath made him mad.
            I am sorry that with better heed and judgement
            I had not quoted him. I feared he did but trifle
            And meant to wrack thee; but beshrew my jealousy!   110
            By heaven, it is as proper to our age
            To cast beyond ourselves in our opinions
            As it is common for the younger sort
            To lack discretion. Come, go we to the King.
            This must be known, which, being kept close,
                                                might move
            More grief to hide, than hate to utter love.[36]
            Come.

                                                [Exeunt.

                        SCENE 2.

            A flourish of trumpets. Enter KING and QUEEN,
            ROSENCRANTZ, GUILDENSTERN, and ATTENDANTS.

KING   Welcome, dear Rosencrantz and Guildenstern!
            Moreover that we much did long to see you,
            The need we have to use you did provoke
            Our hasty sending. Something have you heard
            Of Hamlet's transformation – so I call it,
            Sith nor th'exterior nor the inward man
            Resembles that it was. What it should be,
            More than his father's death, that thus hath put him
            So much from th'understanding of himself,

I cannot dream of. I entreat you both,   10
That being of so young days brought up with him,
And sith so neighboured to his youth and haviour,
That you vouchsafe your rest here in our court
Some little time, so by your companies
To draw him on to pleasures, and to gather
So much as from occasion you may glean,
Whether aught to us unknown afflicts him thus,
That, opened, lies within our remedy.

QUEEN   Good gentlemen, he hath much talked of you,
And sure I am two men there are not living   20
To whom he more adheres. If it will please you
To show us so much gentry and good will
As to expend your time with us awhile
For the supply and profit of our hope,
Your visitation shall receive such thanks
As fits a king's remembrance.

ROSENCR.   Both your Majesties
Might, by the sovereign power you have of us,
Put your dread pleasures more into command
Than to entreaty.

GUILDEN.   But we both obey,
And here give up ourselves in the full bent,   30
To lay our service freely at your feet
To be commanded.

KING   Thanks Rosencrantz, and gentle Guildenstern.

QUEEN   Thanks Guildenstern, and gentle Rosencrantz;
And I beseech you instantly to visit
My too much changèd son. Go, some of you,
And bring these gentlemen where Hamlet is.

GUILDEN.   Heavens make our presence and our practices
Pleasant and helpful to him!

QUEEN   Ay, amen!
                    [Exeunt Rosencrantz, Guildenstern
                                and some attendants.

                    Enter POLONIUS.[37]

POLONIUS   Th'ambassadors from Norway, my good lord,   40
Are joyfully returned.

KING   Thou still hast been the father of good news.
POLONIUS   Have I, my lord? Assure you, my good liege,
            I hold my duty as I hold my soul,
            Both to my God and to my gracious King;
            And I do think – or else this brain of mine
            Hunts not the trail of policy so sure
            As it hath used to do – that I have found
            The very cause of Hamlet's lunacy.
KING   O speak of that: that do I long to hear.   50
POLONIUS   Give first admittance to th'ambassadors.
            My news shall be the fruit to that great feast.
KING   Thyself do grace to them, and bring them in.

                                                    [*Exit Polonius.*

            He tells me, my dear Gertrude, he hath found
            The head and source of all your son's distemper.
QUEEN   I doubt it is no other but the main:
            His father's death and our o'erhasty marriage.
KING   Well, we shall sift him.

            Enter POLONIUS, VOLTEMAND *and* CORNELIUS.

                                    Welcome, my good friends!
            Say Voltemand, what from our brother Norway?
VOLTEM.   Most fair return of greetings and desires.   60
            Upon our first, he sent out to suppress
            His nephew's levies, which to him appeared
            To be a preparation 'gainst the Polack;
            But better looked into, he truly found
            It was against your Highness; whereat, grieved
            That so his sickness, age and impotence
            Was falsely borne in hand, sends out arrests
            On Fortinbras; which he (in brief) obeys,
            Receives rebuke from Norway, and, in fine,
            Makes vow before his uncle never more   70
            To give th'assay of arms against your Majesty:
            Whereon old Norway, overcome with joy,
            Gives him three thousand crowns in annual fee,
            And his commission to employ those soldiers,
            So levied, as before, against the Polack;
            With an entreaty, herein further shown,
            That it might please you to give quiet pass

Through your dominions for this enterprise,
On such regards of safety and allowance
As therein are set down.   [*He proffers a paper.*

KING   [*taking it:*]   It likes us well,   80
And at our more considered time, we'll read,
Answer, and think upon this business.
Meantime, we thank you for your well-took labour.
Go to your rest; at night we'll feast together.
Most welcome home!
                    [*Exeunt Voltemand, Cornelius and last attendants.*

POLONIUS   This business is well ended.
My liege and madam, to expostulate
What majesty should be, what duty is,
Why day is day, night night, and time is time,
Were nothing but to waste night, day and time.
Therefore, since brevity is the soul of wit,   90
And tediousness the limbs and outward flourishes,
I will be brief. Your noble son is mad.
'Mad' call I it, for to define true madness,
What is't but to be nothing else but mad?
But let that go.

QUEEN   More matter, with less art.

POLONIUS Madam, I swear I use no art at all.
That he is mad, 'tis true; 'tis true, 'tis pity;
And pity 'tis 'tis true. A foolish figure,[38]
But farewell it, for I will use no art.
Mad let us grant him then; and now remains   100
That we find out the cause of this effect,
Or rather say, the cause of this defect,
For this effect defective comes by cause:
Thus it remains, and the remainder thus.
Perpend.   [*He produces a letter.*
I have a daughter – have while she is mine –
Who in her duty and obedience, mark,
Hath given me this. Now gather and surmise.
'To the celestial, and my soul's idol, the most beautified
Ophelia,' – That's an ill phrase, a vile phrase, 'beautified' 110
is a vile phrase, but you shall hear. Thus: 'In her excellent
white bosom, these', etc. –

QUEEN   Came this from Hamlet to her?
POLONIUS   Good madam, stay awhile, I will be faithful.
          'Doubt thou the stars are fire,
            Doubt that the sun doth move,
            Doubt truth to be a liar,
              But never doubt I love.[39]
          O dear Ophelia, I am ill at these numbers, I have not art
          to reckon my groans, but that I love thee best, O most 120
          best, believe it. Adieu.
              Thine evermore, most dear lady, whilst this ma-
              chine is to him, Hamlet.'
          This in obedience hath my daughter shown me,
          And, more above, hath his solicitings,
          As they fell out by time, by means, and place,
          All given to mine ear.
KING   But how hath she
          Received his love?
POLONIUS   What do you think of me ?
KING   As of a man faithful and honourable.
POLONIUS   I would fain prove so. But what might you think,   130
          When I had seen this hot love on the wing,
          As I perceived it (I must tell you that)
          Before my daughter told me – what might you
          Or my dear Majesty your Queen here think,
          If I had played the desk or table-book,
          Or given my heart a working mute and dumb,[40]
          Or looked upon this love with idle sight –
          What might you think? No, I went round to work,
          And my young mistress thus I did bespeak:
          'Lord Hamlet is a prince out of thy star;   140
          This must not be'. And then I prescripts gave her
          That she should lock herself from his resort,
          Admit no messengers, receive no tokens;
          Which done, she took the fruits of my advice:
          And he, repulsèd – a short tale to make –
          Fell into a sadness, then into a fast,
          Thence to a watch, thence into a weakness,
          Thence to a lightness, and, by this declension,
          Into the madness wherein now he raves,

And all we mourn for.

KING   Do you think 'tis this?   150

QUEEN   It may be, very likely.

POLONIUS Hath there been such a time – I'd fain know that –
          That I have positively said ''Tis so',
          When it proved otherwise?

KING   Not that I know.

POLONIUS [pointing to his head and neck:]
          Take this from this, if this be otherwise.
          If circumstances lead me, I will find
          Where truth is hid, though it were hid indeed
          Within the centre.

KING   How may we try it further?

POLONIUS You know sometimes he walks four hours together
          Here in the lobby.

QUEEN   So he does, indeed.   160

POLONIUS At such a time I'll loose my daughter to him.
          Be you and I behind an arras then;
          Mark the encounter. If he love her not,
          And be not from his reason fall'n thereon,
          Let me be no assistant for a state,
          But keep a farm and carters.

KING   We will try it.

                   Enter HAMLET, *reading a book.*

QUEEN   But look where sadly the poor wretch comes reading.

POLONIUS Away, I do beseech you both, away.
          I'll board him presently. O give me leave.
                              [*Exeunt King and Queen.*
          How does my good Lord Hamlet?   170

HAMLET   Well, God-a-mercy.

POLONIUS Do you know me, my lord?

HAMLET   Excellent well: you are a fishmonger.[41]

POLONIUS Not I, my lord.

HAMLET   Then I would you were so honest a man.

POLONIUS Honest, my lord?

HAMLET   Ay sir. To be honest, as this world goes, is to be one
          man picked out of ten thousand.

POLONIUS That's very true, my lord.

HAMLET	For if the sun breed maggots in a dead dog, being a 180
	good kissing carrion – Have you a daughter?
POLONIUS	I have, my lord.
HAMLET	Let her not walk i'th'sun. Conception is a blessing; but
	as your daughter may conceive – friend look to't.[42]

[*He reads again.*

POLONIUS [*aside:*] How say you by that? Still harping on my
daughter. Yet he knew me not at first: he said I was a
fishmonger. He is far gone, far gone; and truly, in my
youth, I suffered much extremity for love, very near
this. I'll speak to him again. – What do you read, my lord?

HAMLET   Words, words, words.   190

POLONIUS What is the matter, my lord?

HAMLET   Between who?

POLONIUS I mean the matter that you read, my lord.

HAMLET   Slanders, sir; for the satirical rogue says here that old
men have grey beards, that their faces are wrinkled,
their eyes purging thick amber and plum-tree gum,
and that they have a plentiful lack of wit, together
with most weak hams – all which, sir, though I most
powerfully and potently believe, yet I hold it not
honesty to have it thus set down; for yourself, sir, shall 200
grow old as I am, if like a crab you could go backward.

[*He reads again.*

POLONIUS [*aside:*] Though this be madness, yet there is method
in't. – Will you walk out of the air, my lord?

HAMLET   Into my grave.

POLONIUS [*aside:*] Indeed, that's out of the air; how pregnant
sometimes his replies are! A happiness that often madness
hits on, which reason and sanity could not so prosper-
ously be delivered of. I will leave him, and suddenly
contrive the means of meeting between him and my
daughter. – My honourable lord, I will most humbly 210
take my leave of you.

HAMLET   You cannot, sir, take from me anything that I will
more willingly part withal: except my life, except my
life, except my life.

POLONIUS Fare you well, my lord.

HAMLET   These tedious old fools!

Enter ROSENCRANTZ *and* GUILDENSTERN.

POLONIUS	You go to seek the Lord Hamlet. There he is.
ROSENCR.	[*to Polonius:*] God save you, sir! [*Exit Polonius.*
GUILDEN.	My honoured lord!
ROSENCR.	My most dear lord! 220
HAMLET	My excellent good friends! How dost thou, Guilden-stern? Ah, Rosencrantz! Good lads, how do you both?
ROSENCR.	As the indifferent children of the earth.
GUILDEN.	Happy, in that we are not over-happy,
	On Fortune's cap we are not the very button.
HAMLET	Nor the soles of her shoe?
ROSENCR.	Neither, my lord.
HAMLET	Then you live about her waist or in the middle of her favours?
GUILDEN.	Faith, her privates we. 230
HAMLET	In the secret parts of Fortune? O, most true: she is a strumpet. What's the news?
ROSENCR.	None, my lord, but that the world's grown honest.
HAMLET	Then is doomsday near; but your news is not true. Let me question more in particular: what have you, my good friends, deserved at the hands of Fortune, that she sends you to prison hither?
GUILDEN.	Prison, my lord?
HAMLET	Denmark's a prison.
ROSENCR.	Then is the world one. 240
HAMLET	A goodly one, in which there are many confines, wards and dungeons; Denmark being one o'th'worst.
ROSENCR.	We think not so, my lord.
HAMLET	Why, then 'tis none to you; for there is nothing either good or bad, but thinking makes it so. To me it is a prison.
ROSENCR..	Why, then your ambition makes it one: 'tis too narrow for your mind.
HAMLET	O God! I could be bounded in a nut-shell, and count myself a king of infinite space; were it not that I have 250 bad dreams.
GUILDEN.	Which dreams, indeed, are ambition: for the very substance of the ambitious is merely the shadow of a dream.

HAMLET   A dream itself is but a shadow.

ROSENCR.   Truly, and I hold ambition of so airy and light a
            quality, that it is but a shadow's shadow.

HAMLET   Then are our beggars bodies, and our monarchs and
            outstretched heroes the beggars' shadows.⁴³ Shall we to
            th'court? For, by my fay, I cannot reason.   260

ROSENCR., GUILDEN. We'll wait upon you.

HAMLET   No such matter: I will not sort you with the rest of my
            servants; for to speak to you like an honest man, I am
            most dreadfully attended.⁴⁴ But, in the beaten way of
            friendship, what make you at Elsinore?

ROSENCR.   To visit you, my lord, no other occasion.

HAMLET   Beggar that I am, I am even poor in thanks, but I thank
            you; and sure, dear friends, my thanks are too dear a
            halfpenny. Were you not sent for? Is it your own
            inclining? Is it a free visitation? Come, come, deal   270
            justly with me: come, come; nay speak.

GUILDEN.   What should we say, my lord?

HAMLET   Why, anything but to th'purpose. You were sent for;
            and there is a kind of confession in your looks, which
            your modesties have not craft enough to colour. I
            know the good King and Queen have sent for you.

ROSENCR.   To what end, my lord?

HAMLET   That you must teach me. But let me conjure you, by
            the rights of our fellowship, by the consonancy of our
            youth, by the obligation of our ever-preserved love,   280
            and by what more dear a better proposer can charge
            you withal, be even and direct with me whether you
            were sent for or no.

ROSENCR.   [aside to Guildenstern:] What say you?

HAMLET   Nay then, I have an eye of you. If you love me, hold
            not off.

GUILDEN.   My lord, we were sent for.

HAMLET   I will tell you why. So shall my anticipation prevent
            your discovery, and your secrecy to the King and Queen
            moult no feather. I have of late, but wherefore I know   290
            not, lost all my mirth, forgone all custom of exercise;
            and indeed, it goes so heavily with my disposition,
            that this goodly frame, the earth, seems to me a sterile

promontory; this most excellent canopy, the air, look you, this brave o'erhanging firmament, this majestical roof fretted with golden fire – why, it appeareth nothing to me but a foul and pestilent congregation of vapours. What a piece of work is a man: how noble in reason, how infinite in faculties; in form and moving, how express and admirable; in action, how like an angel; in apprehension, 300 how like a god; the beauty of the world; the paragon of animals; and yet, to me, what is this quintessence of dust? Man delights not me – no, nor woman neither, though by your smiling you seem to say so.

ROSENCR.   My lord, there was no such stuff in my thoughts.

HAMLET   Why did ye laugh then, when I said 'man delights not me'?

ROSENCR.   To think, my lord, if you delight not in man, what Lenten entertainment the players shall receive from you. We coted them on the way, and hither are they 310 coming to offer you service.

HAMLET   He that plays the King shall be welcome. His Majesty shall have tribute of me, the adventurous Knight shall use his foil and target, the Lover shall not sigh gratis, the Humorous Man shall end his part in peace, the Clown shall make those laugh whose lungs are tickle o'th'sere, and the Lady shall say her mind freely – or the blank verse shall halt for't.[45] What players are they?

ROSENCR.   Even those you were wont to take such delight in: the tragedians of the city. 320

HAMLET   How chances it they travel? Their residence, both in reputation and profit, was better; both ways.

ROSENCR.   I think their inhibition comes by the means of the late innovation.[46]

HAMLET   Do they hold the same estimation they did when I was in the city? Are they so followed?

ROSENCR.   No, indeed, they are not.

HAMLET   How comes it? Do they grow rusty?

ROSENCR.   Nay, their endeavour keeps in the wonted pace; but there is, sir, an eyrie of children;[47] little eyases, that cry 330 out on the top of question, and are most tyrannically clapped for't. These are now the fashion, and so

berattle the common stages (so they call them) that
many wearing rapiers are afraid of goose-quills, and
dare scarce come thither.

HAMLET   What, are they children? Who maintains 'em? How are
          they escoted? Will they pursue the quality no longer
          than they can sing? Will they not say afterwards, if they
          should grow themselves to common players (as it is like
          most will if their means are no better), their writers do 340
          them wrong, to make them exclaim against their own
          succession?

ROSENCR. Faith, there has been much to-do on both sides; and
          the nation holds it no sin to tar them to controversy.
          There was, for a while, no money bid for argument,
          unless the poet and the player went to cuffs in the
          question.

HAMLET   Is't possible?

GUILDEN. O, there has been much throwing about of brains.

HAMLET   Do the boys carry it away?   350

ROSENCR. Ay, that they do, my lord; Hercules and his load too.[48]

HAMLET   It is not very strange, for my uncle is King of Denmark,
          and those that would make mouths at him while my
          father lived, give twenty, forty, fifty, a hundred ducats
          apiece for his picture in little. 'Sblood, there is some-
          thing in this more than natural, if philosophy could
          find it out.   [A flourish of trumpets heard.

GUILDEN. There are the players.

HAMLET   Gentlemen, you are welcome to Elsinore. Your
          hands. Come then. Th'appurtenance of welcome is 360
          fashion and ceremony; let me comply with you in this
          garb [he shakes their hands], lest my extent to the
          players, which I tell you must show fairly outwards,
          should more appear like entertainment than yours.
          You are welcome; but my uncle-father, and aunt-
          mother, are deceived.

GUILDEN. In what, my dear lord?

HAMLET   I am but mad north-north-west; when the wind is
          southerly, I know a hawk from a handsaw.[49]

                          Enter POLONIUS.

POLONIUS	Well be with you, gentlemen.	370

HAMLET   Hark you Guildenstern, and you too – at each ear a
          hearer: that great baby you see there is not yet out of
          his swaddling-clouts.

ROSENCR. Happily he is the second time come to them, for they
          say an old man is twice a child.

HAMLET   I will prophesy: he comes to tell me of the players.
          Mark it. – You say right sir, a Monday morning, 'twas
          then indeed.

POLONIUS My lord, I have news to tell you.

HAMLET   My lord, I have news to tell you. When Roscius was an   380
          actor in Rome –

POLONIUS The actors are come hither, my lord.

HAMLET   Buzz, buzz!

POLONIUS Upon my honour –

HAMLET   'Then came each actor on his ass' –

POLONIUS The best actors in the world, either for tragedy,
          comedy, history, pastoral, pastoral-comical, historical-
          pastoral, tragical-historical, tragical-comical-historical-
          pastoral, scene individable, or poem unlimited.⁵⁰ Seneca
          cannot be too heavy, nor Plautus too light.⁵¹ For the   390
          law of writ and the liberty,⁵² these are the only men.

HAMLET   O Jephthah,⁵³ judge of Israel, what a treasure hadst thou!

POLONIUS What a treasure had he, my lord?

HAMLET   Why,
                 'One fair daughter, and no more,
                     The which he lovèd passing well.'

POLONIUS [aside:] Still on my daughter.

HAMLET   Am I not i'th' right, old Jephthah?

POLONIUS If you call me Jephthah, my lord, I have a daughter that
          I love passing well.   400

HAMLET   Nay, that follows not.

POLONIUS What follows then, my lord?

HAMLET   Why,
                     'As by lot, God wot',
          and then, you know,
                     'It came to pass, as most like it was.'
          The first row of the pious chanson will show you
          more, for look where my abridgement comes.

Enter four or five PLAYERS.

You are welcome masters, welcome all! – I am glad to
see thee well. – Welcome, good friends! – O, my old   410
friend! Why, thy face is valanced since I saw thee last:
com'st thou to beard me in Denmark? – What, my
young lady and mistress! By'r lady, your ladyship is
nearer to heaven than when I saw you last by the
altitude of a chopine. Pray God your voice, like a piece
of uncurrent gold, be not cracked within the ring.
Masters, you are all welcome. We'll e'en to't like
French falconers – fly at anything we see. We'll have a
speech straight. [*To the First Player:*] Come, give us a
taste of your quality: come, a passionate speech.   420

PLAYER I   What speech, my good lord?

HAMLET   I heard thee speak me a speech once, but it was never
acted; or if it was, not above once, for the play I
remember pleased not the million; 'twas caviare to the
general, but it was (as I received it, and others, whose
judgements in such matters cried in the top of mine) an
excellent play, well digested in the scenes, set down
with as much modesty as cunning. I remember one said
there were no sallets in the lines, to make the matter
savoury, nor no matter in the phrase that might indict   430
the author of affectation, but called it an honest method,
as wholesome as sweet, and, by very much, more handsome than fine.[54] One speech in't I chiefly loved, 'twas
Aeneas' tale to Dido, and thereabout of it especially
where he speaks of Priam's slaughter.[55] If it live in your
memory, begin at this line – let me see, let me see –
'The rugged Pyrrhus, like th'Hyrcanian beast' –
'tis not so; it begins with Pyrrhus –
   'The rugged Pyrrhus, he whose sable arms,
   Black as his purpose, did the night resemble   440
   When he lay couchèd in the ominous horse,[56]
   Hath now this dread and black complexion smeared
   With heraldry more dismal: head to foot
   Now is he total gules, horridly tricked
   With blood of fathers, mothers, daughters, sons,
   Baked and impasted with the parching streets,

> That lend a tyrannous and a damned light
> To their lord's murder. Roasted in wrath and fire,
> And thus o'er-sizèd with coagulate gore,
> With eyes like carbuncles, the hellish Pyrrhus   450
> Old grandsire Priam seeks.'
> So proceed you.

POLONIUS 'Fore God, my lord, well spoken, with good accent and
good discretion.

PLAYER I   'Anon he finds him
> Striking too short at Greeks; his antique sword,
> Rebellious to his arm, lies where it falls,
> Repugnant to command. Unequal matched,
> Pyrrhus at Priam drives, in rage strikes wide,
> But with the whiff and wind of his fell sword   460
> Th'unnervèd father falls. Then senseless Ilium,[57]
> Seeming to feel this blow, with flaming top
> Stoops to his base, and with a hideous crash
> Takes prisoner Pyrrhus' ear. For lo! his sword,
> Which was declining on the milky head
> Of reverend Priam, seemed i'th'air to stick;
> So, as a painted tyrant, Pyrrhus stood,
> And like a neutral to his will and matter,
> Did nothing.
> But as we often see, against some storm,   470
> A silence in the heavens, the rack stand still,
> The bold winds speechless, and the orb below
> As hush as death, anon the dreadful thunder
> Doth rend the region; so after Pyrrhus' pause,
> A rousèd vengeance sets him new awork;
> And never did the Cyclops' hammers fall
> On Mars's armour, forged for proof eterne,
> With less remorse than Pyrrhus' bleeding sword
> Now falls on Priam.
> Out, out, thou strumpet Fortune![58] All you gods,   480
> In general synod take away her power,
> Break all the spokes and fellies from her wheel,
> And bowl the round nave down the hill of heaven
> As low as to the fiends!'

POLONIUS This is too long.

HAMLET   It shall to the barber's, with your beard. – Prithee say
          on; he's for a jig, or a tale of bawdry, or he sleeps; say
          on, come to Hecuba.

PLAYER I 'But who, ah woe! had seen the mobled queen' –

HAMLET   'The mobled queen'?   490

POLONIUS That's good, 'mobled queen' is good.

PLAYER I 'Run barefoot up and down, threat'ning the flames
          With bisson rheum, a clout upon that head
          Where late the diadem stood, and, for a robe,
          About her lank and all o'er-teemèd loins,
          A blanket in the alarm of fear caught up –
          Who this had seen, with tongue in venom steeped,
          'Gainst Fortune's state would treason have
                                                 pronounced;
          But if the gods themselves did see her then,
          When she saw Pyrrhus make malicious sport   500
          In mincing with his sword her husband's limbs,
          The instant burst of clamour that she made
          (Unless things mortal move them not at all)
          Would have made milch the burning eyes of heaven,
          And passion in the gods.'

POLONIUS Look whe'r he has not turned his colour and has tears
          in's eyes. – Prithee no more.

HAMLET   'Tis well; I'll have thee speak out the rest of this soon.
          – Good my lord, will you see the players well be-
          stowed? Do you hear? Let them be well used, for they   510
          are the abstracts and brief chronicles of the time. After
          your death you were better have a bad epitaph than
          their ill report while you live.

POLONIUS My lord, I will use them according to their desert.

HAMLET   God's bodkin, man, much better! Use every man after
          his desert, and who shall scape whipping? Use them after
          your own honour and dignity: the less they deserve, the
          more merit is in your bounty. Take them in.

POLONIUS Come, sirs.   [He goes to the door.

HAMLET   Follow him, friends; we'll hear a play tomorrow. [He   520
          stops the First Player.] Dost thou hear me, old friend,
          can you play The Murder of Gonzago?

PLAYER 1	Ay, my lord.
HAMLET	We'll ha't tomorrow night. You could for a need study a speech of some dozen or sixteen lines, which I would set down and insert in't, could you not?
PLAYER 1	Ay, my lord.
HAMLET	Very well. Follow that lord, and look you mock him not. [*Exeunt Polonius and the Players. To Rosencrantz and Guildenstern:*] My good friends, I'll leave you till night. 530 You are welcome to Elsinore.
ROSENCR.	Good my lord. [*Exeunt Rosencrantz and Guildenstern.*
HAMLET	Ay, so, God buy you! Now I am alone.

O, what a rogue and peasant slave am I!
Is it not monstrous that this player here,
But in a fiction, in a dream of passion,
Could force his soul so to his own conceit
That from her working[59] all his visage wanned,
Tears in his eyes, distraction in's aspéct,
A broken voice, and his whole function suiting   540
With forms to his conceit; and all for nothing!
For Hecuba!
What's Hecuba to him, or he to Hecuba,
That he should weep for her? What would he do,
Had he the motive and the cue for passion
That I have? He would drown the stage with tears,
And cleave the general ear with horrid speech,
Make mad the guilty and appal the free,
Confound the ignorant, and amaze indeed
The very faculties of eyes and ears. Yet I,   *550
A dull and muddy-mettled rascal, peak
Like John-a-dreams, unpregnant of my cause,
And can say nothing; no, not for a king,
Upon whose property and most dear life
A damned defeat was made. Am I a coward?
Who calls me villain, breaks my pate across,
Plucks off my beard and blows it in my face,
Tweaks me by th'nose, gives me the lie i'th'throat
As deep as to the lungs – who does me this,
Ha? 'Swounds, I should take it: for it cannot be   560
But I am pigeon-livered, and lack gall

To make oppression bitter, or ere this
I should have fatted all the region kites
With this slave's offal. Bloody, bawdy villain!
Remorseless, treacherous, lecherous, kindless villain!
O, vengeance!
Why, what an ass am I! This is most brave,
That I, the son of a dear father murdered,[60]
Prompted to my revenge by heaven and hell,
Must like a whore unpack my heart with words,   570
And fall a-cursing like a very drab,
A scullion! Fie upon't; foh!
About, my brains. Hum . . . I have heard
That guilty creatures, sitting at a play,
Have by the very cunning of the scene
Been struck so to the soul, that presently
They have proclaimed their malefactions:
For murder, though it have no tongue, will speak
With most miraculous organ. I'll have these players
Play something like the murder of my father,   580
Before mine uncle. I'll observe his looks;
I'll tent him to the quick. If he but blench,
I know my course. The spirit that I have seen
May be the devil,[61] and the devil hath power
T'assume a pleasing shape; yea, and perhaps
Out of my weakness and my melancholy,
As he is very potent with such spirits,[62]
Abuses me to damn me. I'll have grounds
More relative than this. The play's the thing
Wherein I'll catch the conscience of the King.   590

[Exit.

ACT 3, SCENE 1.

Enter KING, QUEEN, POLONIUS, OPHELIA,
ROSENCRANTZ *and* GUILDENSTERN.

KING   And can you by no drift of circumstance[63]
          Get from him why he puts on this confusion,
          Grating so harshly all his days of quiet
          With turbulent and dangerous lunacy?

ROSENCR. He does confess he feels himself distracted,
          But from what cause he will by no means speak.

GUILDEN. Nor do we find him forward to be sounded,
          But with a crafty madness keeps aloof
          When we would bring him on to some confession
          Of his true state.

QUEEN   Did he receive you well?   10

ROSENCR. Most like a gentleman.

GUILDEN. But with much forcing of his disposition.

ROSENCR. Niggard of question, but of our demands
          Most free in his reply.

QUEEN   Did you assay him
          To any pastime?

ROSENCR. Madam, it so fell out that certain players
          We o'er-raught on the way. Of these we told him,
          And there did seem in him a kind of joy
          To hear of it. They are here about the court,
          And, as I think, they have already order   20
          This night to play before him.

POLONIUS   'Tis most true;
          And he beseeched me to entreat your Majesties
          To hear and see the matter.

KING   With all my heart, and it doth much content me
          To hear him so inclined.
          Good gentlemen, give him a further edge,
          And drive his purpose into these delights.

ROSENCR. We shall, my lord.
                          [*Exeunt Rosencrantz and Guildenstern.*

KING   Sweet Gertrude, leave us too,

For we have closely sent for Hamlet hither,
That he, as 'twere by accident, may here   30
Affront Ophelia.
Her father and myself (lawful espials)
Will so bestow ourselves, that seeing unseen,
We may of their encounter frankly judge,
And gather by him, as he is behaved,
If't be th'affliction of his love or no
That thus he suffers for.

QUEEN   I shall obey you; –
And for your part, Ophelia, I do wish
That your good beauties be the happy cause
Of Hamlet's wildness; so shall I hope your virtues   40
Will bring him to his wonted way again,
To both your honours.

OPHELIA   Madam, I wish it may.
                                        [Exit Queen.

POLONIUS Ophelia, walk you here. – Gracious, so please you,
We will bestow ourselves. – Read on this book,
That show of such an exercise may colour
Your loneliness. We are oft to blame in this,
'Tis too much proved, that with devotion's visage
And pious action we do sugar o'er
The devil himself.

KING   [aside:]   O, 'tis too true:
How smart a lash that speech doth give my conscience!   50
The harlot's cheek, beautied with plast'ring art,
Is not more ugly to the thing that helps it
Than is my deed to my most painted word:
O heavy burden!

POLONIUS I hear him coming; let's withdraw, my lord.
                                [Exeunt King and Polonius.

                    Enter HAMLET.

HAMLET   To be, or not to be: that is the question:
Whether 'tis nobler in the mind to suffer
The slings and arrows of outrageous fortune,
Or to take arms against a sea of troubles,
And, by opposing, end them. To die – to sleep,   60

No more; and by a sleep to say we end
The heart-ache and the thousand natural shocks
That flesh is heir to: 'tis a consummation
Devoutly to be wished. To die, to sleep;
To sleep, perchance to dream. Ay, there's the rub,
For in that sleep of death what dreams may come,
When we have shuffled off this mortal coil,
Must give us pause. There's the respect
That makes calamity of so long life;
For who would bear the whips and scorns of time,   70
Th'oppressor's wrong, the proud man's contumely,
The pangs of disprized love, the law's delay,
The insolence of office, and the spurns
That patient merit of th'unworthy takes,
When he himself might his quietus make
With a bare bodkin? Who would fardels bear,
To grunt and sweat under a weary life,
But that the dread of something after death
(The undiscovered country, from whose bourn
No traveller returns) puzzles the will,   80
And makes us rather bear those ills we have,
Than fly to others that we know not of?
Thus conscience does make cowards of us all;
And thus the native hue of resolution
Is sicklied o'er with the pale cast of thought,
And enterprises of great pitch and moment[64]
With this regard their currents turn awry,
And lose the name of action. – Soft you now,
The fair Ophelia! – Nymph, in thy orisons
Be all my sins remembered.

OPHELIA   Good my lord,   90
How does your honour for this many a day?

HAMLET   I humbly thank you, well, well, well.

OPHELIA   My lord, I have remembrances of yours,
That I have longèd long to re-deliver.
I pray you now receive them.

HAMLET   No, not I;
I never gave you aught.

OPHELIA   My honoured lord, you know right well you did,

And with them words of so sweet breath composed
As made the things more rich. Their perfume lost,
Take these again; for, to the noble mind,   100
Rich gifts wax poor when givers prove unkind.
There, my lord.   [*She gives them to him.*

HAMLET   Ha, ha! Are you honest?

OPHELIA   My lord?

HAMLET   Are you fair?

OPHELIA   What means your lordship?

HAMLET   That if you be honest and fair, your honesty should
admit no discourse to your beauty.

OPHELIA   Could beauty, my lord, have better commerce than
with honesty?   110

HAMLET   Ay truly, for the power of beauty will sooner transform
honesty from what it is to a bawd, than the force of
honesty can translate beauty into his likeness. This was
sometime a paradox, but now the time gives it proof. I
did love you once.

OPHELIA   Indeed, my lord, you made me believe so.

HAMLET   You should not have believed me, for virtue cannot so
inoculate our old stock, but we shall relish of it. I loved
you not.[65]

OPHELIA   I was the more deceived.   120

HAMLET   Get thee to a nunnery. Why wouldst thou be a breeder
of sinners? I am myself indifferent honest, but yet I
could accuse me of such things, that it were better my
mother had not borne me: I am very proud, revengeful,
ambitious, with more offences at my beck than I have
thoughts to put them in, imagination to give them
shape, or time to act them in. What should such fellows
as I do, crawling between earth and heaven? We are
arrant knaves all; believe none of us. Go thy ways to a
nunnery. Where's your father?   130

OPHELIA   At home, my lord.

HAMLET   Let the doors be shut upon him, that he may play the
fool nowhere but in's own house. Farewell.

OPHELIA   O help him, you sweet heavens!

HAMLET   If thou dost marry, I'll give thee this plague for thy
dowry: be thou as chaste as ice, as pure as snow, thou

shalt not escape calumny. Get thee to a nunnery; go,
farewell. Or if thou wilt needs marry, marry a fool, for
wise men know well enough what monsters you make
of them, To a nunnery go, and quickly too. Farewell.   140

OPHELIA   O heavenly powers, restore him!

HAMLET   I have heard of your paintings too, well enough. God
hath given you one face, and you make yourselves
another. You jig, you amble, and you lisp; you nickname God's creatures, and make your wantonness
your ignorance. Go to, I'll no more on't, it hath made
me mad. I say we will have no more marriages. Those
that are married already, all but one, shall live; the rest
shall keep as they are. To a nunnery, go.   [*Exit.*

OPHELIA   O, what a noble mind is here o'erthrown!   .150
The courtier's, soldier's, scholar's, eye, tongue, sword,
Th'expectancy and rose of the fair state,
The glass of fashion and the mould of form,
Th'observed of all observers – quite, quite down!
And I, of ladies most deject and wretched,
That sucked the honey of his music vows,
Now see that noble and most sovereign reason
Like sweet bells jangled out of tune and harsh;
That unmatched form and feature of blown youth
Blasted with ecstasy. O woe is me,   160
T'have seen what I have seen, see what I see!

Enter KING *and* POLONIUS.

KING   Love? His affections do not that way tend;
Nor what he spake, though it lacked form a little,
Was not like madness. There's something in his soul
O'er which his melancholy sits on brood,
And I do doubt the hatch and the disclose
Will be some danger; which for to prevent,
I have in quick determination[66]
Thus set it down: he shall with speed to England,
For the demand of our neglected tribute.[67]   170
Haply the seas, and countries different,
With variable objects, shall expel
This something-settled matter in his heart,

Whereon his brains still beating puts him thus
From fashion of himself. What think you on't?

POLONIUS It shall do well. But yet do I believe
The origin and commencement of his grief
Sprung from neglected love. — How now, Ophelia?
You need not tell us what Lord Hamlet said;
We heard it all. — My lord, do as you please;   180
But if you hold it fit, after the play
Let his queen-mother all alone entreat him
To show his grief; let her be round with him;
And I'll be placed (so please you) in the ear
Of all their conference. If she find him not,
To England send him; or confine him where
Your wisdom best shall think.

KING   It shall be so.
Madness in great ones must not unwatched go.

[Exeunt.

SCENE 2.

Enter HAMLET *and three of the* PLAYERS.

HAMLET   [*to the First Player:*] Speak the speech, I pray you, as I
pronounced it to you, trippingly on the tongue; but if
you mouth it, as many of your players do, I had as lief
the town-crier spoke my lines. Nor do not saw the air
too much with your hand, thus, but use all gently; for in
the very torrent, tempest, and, as I may say, whirlwind
of your passion, you must acquire and beget a
temperance that may give it smoothness. O, it offends
me to the soul, to hear a robustious periwig-pated fellow
tear a passion to tatters, to very rags, to split the ears of 10
the groundlings, who for the most part are capable of
nothing but inexplicable dumb-shows and noise. I
would have such a fellow whipped for o'erdoing
Termagant. It out-Herods Herod. Pray you, avoid it.

PLAYER 1   I warrant your honour.

HAMLET   Be not too tame neither, but let your own discretion
be your tutor. Suit the action to the word, the word to
the action, with this special observance, that you
o'erstep not the modesty of nature: for anything so
o'erdone is from the purpose of playing, whose end, 20
both at the first and now, was and is, to hold, as 'twere,
the mirror up to nature; to show virtue her own
feature, scorn her own image, and the very age and
body of the time his form and pressure. Now
this overdone, or come tardy off, though it make the
unskilful laugh, cannot but make the judicious grieve,
the censure of the which one must in your allowance
o'erweigh a whole theatre of others. O, there be
players that I have seen play – and heard others praise,
and that highly – not to speak it profanely, that neither 30
having th'accent of Christians, nor the gait of Christian, pagan, nor man, have so strutted and bellowed,
that I have thought some of nature's journeymen had

made men, and not made them well, they imitated
humanity so abominably.

PLAYER I   I hope we have reformed that indifferently with us, sir.

HAMLET   O, reform it altogether. And let those that play your
clowns speak no more than is set down for them, for
there be of them that will themselves laugh, to set on
some quantity of barren spectators to laugh too,   40
though in the meantime some necessary question of
the play be then to be considered. That's villainous,
and shows a most pitiful ambition in the fool that uses
it.[68] Go, make you ready.

[*Exeunt Players.*

Enter POLONIUS *with* ROSENCRANTZ *and* GUILDENSTERN.

How now, my lord? Will the King hear this piece of
work?

POLONIUS And the Queen too, and that presently.

HAMLET   Bid the players make haste.

[*Exit Polonius.*

Will you two help to hasten them?

ROSENCR. Ay, my lord.   50

[*Exit Rosencrantz and Guildenstern.*

HAMLET   What ho, Horatio!

Enter HORATIO.

HORATIO   Here, sweet lord, at your service.

HAMLET   Horatio, thou art e'en as just a man
As e'er my conversation coped withal.

HORATIO   O, my dear lord, —

HAMLET   Nay, do not think I flatter,
For what advancement may I hope from thee,
That no revénue hast but thy good spirits
To feed and clothe thee? Why should the poor be
                                                      flattered?
No, let the candied tongue lick ábsurd pomp,
And crook the pregnant hinges of the knee   60
Where thrift may follow fawning. Dost thou hear?
Since my dear soul was mistress of her choice,
And could of men distinguish, her election
Hath sealed thee for herself; for thou hast been

As one, in suff'ring all, that suffers nothing;
A man that Fortune's buffets and rewards
Hath ta'en with equal thanks; and blest are those
Whose blood and judgement are so well co-mingled
That they are not a pipe for Fortune's finger
To sound what stop she please. Give me that man   70
That is not passion's slave, and I will wear him
In my heart's core, ay, in my heart of heart,
As I do thee. Something too much of this.
There is a play tonight before the King:
One scene of it comes near the circumstance
Which I have told thee of my father's death.
I prithee, when thou seest that act afoot,
Even with the very comment of thy soul
Observe my uncle. If his occulted guilt
Do not itself unkennel in one speech,   80
It is a damnèd ghost that we have seen,
And my imaginations are as foul
As Vulcan's stithy. Give him heedful note,
For I mine eyes will rivet to his face,
And, after, we will both our judgements join
In censure of his seeming.

HORATIO   Well, my lord.
If he steal aught the whilst this play is playing,
And scape detecting, I will pay the theft.
                 [*Trumpets and kettle-drums heard.*

HAMLET   They are coming to the play. I must be idle.
Get you a place.   90

Enter KING, QUEEN, POLONIUS, OPHELIA,
ROSENCRANTZ, GUILDENSTERN, *and* LORDS *attendant,*
with the King's GUARD *carrying torches. A Danish*
march is followed by a flourish of trumpets.

KING   How fares our cousin Hamlet?
HAMLET   Excellent i'faith, of the chameleon's dish. I eat the air,
promise-crammed; you cannot feed capons so.
KING   I have nothing with this answer, Hamlet. These words
are not mine.

HAMLET	No, nor mine now. [*To Polonius:*] My lord, you played once i'th'university, you say?
POLONIUS	That did I, my lord, and was accounted a good actor.
HAMLET	What did you enact?
POLONIUS	I did enact Julius Caesar. I was killed i'th'Capitol: 100 Brutus killed me.
HAMLET	It was a brute part of him to kill so capital a calf there. Be the players ready?
ROSENCR.	Ay, my lord, they stay upon your patience.
QUEEN	Come hither, my dear Hamlet, sit by me.
HAMLET	No, good mother, here's metal more attractive.

[*He joins Ophelia.*]

POLONIUS	[*to the King:*] O ho! Do you mark that?
HAMLET	Lady, shall I lie in your lap?
OPHELIA	No, my lord.
HAMLET	I mean, my head upon your lap? 110
OPHELIA	Ay, my lord.
HAMLET	Do you think I meant country matters? [69]
OPHELIA	I think nothing, my lord.
HAMLET	That's a fair thought to lie between maids' legs.
OPHELIA	What is, my lord?
HAMLET	Nothing. [70]
OPHELIA	You are merry, my lord.
HAMLET	Who, I?
OPHELIA	Ay, my lord.
HAMLET	O God, your only jig-maker. What should a man do 120 but be merry? For look you how cheerfully my mother looks, and my father died within's two hours.
OPHELIA	Nay, 'tis twice two months, my lord.
HAMLET	So long? Nay, then let the devil wear black, for I'll have a suit of sables. [71] O heavens, die two months ago, and not forgotten yet? Then there's hope a great man's memory may outlive his life half a year; but by'r Lady he must build churches then, or else shall he suffer not thinking on, with the hobby-horse, whose epitaph is 'For O, for O, the hobby-horse is forgot.' [72] 130

The trumpets sound to herald the Dumb-Show.

The Dumb-Show.

Enter a King and a Queen, very lovingly, the Queen embracing him and he her. She kneels and makes show of protestation unto him. He takes her up and declines his head upon her neck. He lies him down upon a bank of flowers. She, seeing him asleep, leaves him. Anon comes in another man, takes off his crown, kisses it, pours poison in the sleeper's ears, and leaves him. The Queen returns, finds the King dead, and makes passionate action. The poisoner, with some two or three mutes, comes in again, seeming to condole with her. The dead body is carried away. The poisoner woos the Queen with gifts. She seems harsh awhile, but in the end accepts his love.

OPHELIA	What means this, my lord?
HAMLET	Marry, this is miching malicho,[73] it means mischief.
OPHELIA	Belike this show imports the argument of the play.

Enter PLAYER *as Prologue.*

HAMLET	We shall know by this fellow. The players cannot keep counsel: they'll tell all.
OPHELIA	Will he tell us what this show meant?
HAMLET	Ay, or any show that you will show him. Be not you ashamed to show, he'll not shame to tell you what it means.[74]
OPHELIA	You are naught, you are naught. I'll mark the play. 140
PLAYER	For us and for our tragedy,
	Here stooping to your clemency,
	We beg your hearing patiently. [*Exit.*
HAMLET	Is this a prologue, or the posy of a ring?
OPHELIA	'Tis brief, my lord.
HAMLET	As woman's love.

Enter two PLAYERS *as a King and a Queen.*

PL. KING	Full thirty times hath Phoebus' cart gone round
	Neptune's salt wash and Tellus' orbèd ground,
	And thirty dozen moons with borrowed sheen
	About the world have times twelve thirties been, 150
	Since love our hearts and Hymen did our hands
	Unite commutual in most sacred bands.
PL. QUEEN	So many journeys may the sun and moon
	Make us again count o'er ere love be done!

But woe is me, you are so sick of late,
So far from cheer and from your former state,
That I distrust you. Yet though I distrust,
Discomfort you, my lord, it nothing must;
For women fear too much, even as they love,
And women's fear and love hold quantity,   160
In neither aught, or in extremity.[75]
Now what my love is, proof hath made you know,
And as my love is sized, my fear is so.
Where love is great, the littlest doubts are fear;
Where little fears grow great, great love grows there.[76]

PL. KING   Faith, I must leave thee, love, and shortly too.
My operant powers their functions leave to do,
And thou shalt live in this fair world behind,
Honoured, beloved; and haply one as kind
For husband shalt thou –

PL. QUEEN   O, confound the rest!   170
Such love must needs be treason in my breast.
In second husband let me be accurst:
None wed the second, but who killed the first.

HAMLET   That's wormwood, wormwood.

PL. QUEEN   The instances that second marriage move
Are base respects of thrift, but none of love.
A second time I kill my husband dead,
When second husband kisses me in bed.

PL. KING   I do believe you think what now you speak,
But what we do determine, oft we break.   180
Purpose is but the slave to memory,
Of violent birth but poor validity,
Which now like fruit unripe sticks on the tree,
But fall unshaken when they mellow be.
Most necessary 'tis that we forget
To pay ourselves what to ourselves is debt.[77]
What to ourselves in passion we propose,
The passion ending, doth the purpose lose.
The violence of either grief or joy
Their own enactures with themselves destroy.   190
Where joy most revels, grief doth most lament;
Grief joys, joy grieves, on slender accident.

	This world is not for aye, nor 'tis not strange	
	That even our loves should with our fortunes change;	
	For 'tis a question left us yet to prove,	
	Whether love lead fortune, or else fortune love.	
	The great man down, you mark his favourite flies;	
	The poor, advanced, makes friends of enemies;	
	And hitherto doth love on fortune tend,	
	For who not needs shall never lack a friend,	200
	And who in want a hollow friend doth try,	
	Directly seasons him his enemy.	
	But orderly to end where I begun:	
	Our wills and fates do so contráry run,	
	That our devices still are overthrown;	
	Our thoughts are ours, their ends none of our own.	
	So think thou wilt no second husband wed,	
	But die thy thoughts when thy first lord is dead.	
PL. QUEEN	Nor earth to me give food nor heaven light,	
	Sport and repose lock from me day and night,	210
	To desperation turn my trust and hope,	
	An anchor's cheer in prison be my scope;[78]	
	Each opposite that blanks the face of joy	
	Meet what I would have well, and it destroy;	
	Both here and hence pursue me lasting strife,	
	If, once a widow, ever I be wife!	
HAMLET	If she should break it now!	
PL. KING	'Tis deeply sworn. Sweet, leave me here awhile.	
	My spirits grow dull, and fain I would beguile	
	The tedious day with sleep. [*He sleeps.*	
PL. QUEEN	Sleep rock thy brain,	220
	And never come mischance between us twain! [*Exit.*	
HAMLET	Madam, how like you this play?	
QUEEN	The lady doth protest too much, methinks.	
HAMLET	O, but she'll keep her word.	
KING	Have you heard the argument? Is there no offence in't?	
HAMLET	No, no, they do but jest, poison in jest; no offence i'th'world.	
KING	What do you call the play?	
HAMLET	*The Mousetrap*. Marry, how? Tropically.[79] This play is	230

the image of a murder done in Vienna. Gonzago is the
Duke's name, his wife Baptista:[80] you shall see anon.
'Tis a knavish piece of work, but what of that? Your
Majesty, and we that have free souls, it touches us not.
Let the galled jade wince, our withers are unwrung.[81]

Enter PLAYER *as Lucianus.*

This is one Lucianus, nephew to the King.

OPHELIA   You are as good as a chorus, my lord.

HAMLET   I could interpret between you and your love, if I could
see the puppets dallying.[82]

OPHELIA   You are keen, my lord, you are keen.   240

HAMLET   It would cost you a groaning to take off mine edge.

OPHELIA   Still better and worse.[83]

HAMLET   So you mis-take your husbands.[84] – Begin, murderer.
Pox! Leave thy damnable faces and begin! Come – 'the
croaking raven doth bellow for revenge.'[85]

LUCIANUS   Thoughts black, hands apt, drugs fit, and time
                                                    agreeing,
Confederate season, else no creature seeing,
Thou mixture rank, of midnight weeds collected,
With Hecate's ban thrice blasted, thrice infected,
Thy natural magic and dire property   250
On wholesome life usurps immediately.
            [*He pours the poison into the sleeper's ears.*

HAMLET   He poisons him i'th'garden for's estate. His name's
Gonzago: the story is extant, and written in very choice
Italian. You shall see anon how the murderer gets the
love of Gonzago's wife.

OPHELIA   The King rises.

HAMLET   What, frighted with false fire?

QUEEN   How fares my lord?

POLONIUS   Give o'er the play.

KING   Give me some light – away!   260

POLONIUS   Lights, lights, lights!
            [*Exeunt all but Hamlet and Horatio.*

HAMLET   Why, let the stricken deer go weep,
                The hart ungallèd play,
            For some must watch while some must sleep,
                Thus runs the world away.

           Would not this, sir, and a forest of feathers, if the rest of
           my fortunes turn Turk with me, with two Provincial
           roses on my razed shoes, get me a fellowship in a cry of
           players, sir?[86]

HORATIO   Half a share.   270

HAMLET   A whole one, I.
              For thou dost know, O Damon dear,
                This realm dismantled was
              Of Jove himself, and now reigns here
                A very, very – pajock.

HORATIO   You might have rhymed.[87]

HAMLET   O good Horatio, I'll take the ghost's word for a thousand
           pound. Didst perceive?

HORATIO   Very well, my lord.

HAMLET   Upon the talk of the poisoning?   280

HORATIO   I did very well note him.

              Enter ROSENCRANTZ *and* GUILDENSTERN.

HAMLET   Ah, ha! Come, some music! Come, the recorders!
              For if the King like not the comedy,
                Why then, belike, – he likes it not, perdy.
           Come, some music!

GUILDEN.   Good my lord, vouchsafe me a word with you.

HAMLET   Sir, a whole history.

GUILDEN.   The King, sir, –

HAMLET   Ay, sir, what of him?

GUILDEN.   Is in his retirement marvellous distempered.   290

HAMLET   With drink, sir?

GUILDEN.   No my lord, rather with choler.

HAMLET   Your wisdom should show itself more richer to signify
           this to the doctor. For, for me to put him to his
           purgation, would perhaps plunge him into more choler.

GUILDEN.   Good my lord, put your discourse into some frame,
           and start not so wildly from my affair.

HAMLET   I am tame, sir. Pronounce.

GUILDEN.   The Queen your mother, in most great affliction of
           spirit, hath sent me to you.   300

HAMLET   You are welcome.

GUILDEN.   Nay, good my lord, this courtesy is not of the right

breed. If it shall please you to make me a wholesome
answer, I will do your mother's commandment. If not,
your pardon and my return shall be the end of my
business.

HAMLET   Sir, I cannot.

ROSENCR. What, my lord?

HAMLET   Make you a wholesome answer: my wit's diseased. But,
sir, such answer as I can make, you shall command, or 310
rather, as you say, my mother. Therefore no more, but
to the matter. My mother, you say –

ROSENCR. Then thus she says, your behaviour hath struck her
into amazement and admiration.

HAMLET   O wonderful son, that can so astonish a mother! But is
there no sequel at the heels of this mother's admiration?
Impart.

ROSENCR. She desires to speak with you in her closet ere you go
to bed.

HAMLET   We shall obey, were she ten times our mother. Have 320
you any further trade with us?

ROSENCR. My lord, you once did love me.

HAMLET   And do still, by these pickers and stealers.

ROSENCR. Good my lord, what is your cause of distemper? You
do surely bar the door upon your own liberty, if you
deny your griefs to your friend.

HAMLET   Sir, I lack advancement.

ROSENCR. How can that be, when you have the voice of the King
himself for your succession in Denmark?

HAMLET   Ay, sir, but 'While the grass grows' – the proverb is 330
something musty.[88]

Enter PLAYERS *with recorders.*

O, the recorders: let me see one. [*He takes a recorder and
leads Guildenstern aside.*] To withdraw with you, why
do you go about to recover the wind of me, as if you
would drive me into a toil?

GUILDEN.   O, my lord, if my duty be too bold, my love is too
unmannerly.

HAMLET   I do not well understand that – will you play upon this
pipe?

GUILDEN. My lord, I cannot.   340

HAMLET I pray you.

GUILDEN. Believe me, I cannot.

HAMLET I do beseech you.

GUILDEN. I know no touch of it, my lord.

HAMLET It is as easy as lying; govern these ventages with your fingers and thumb, give it breath with your mouth, and it will discourse most eloquent music. Look you, these are the stops.

GUILDEN. But these cannot I command to any utterance of harmony. I have not the skill.   350

HAMLET Why, look you now, how unworthy a thing you make of me! You would play upon me, you would seem to know my stops, you would pluck out the heart of my mystery, you would sound me from my lowest note to the top of my compass; and there is much music, excellent voice, in this little organ, yet cannot you make it speak. 'Sblood, do you think I am easier to be played on than a pipe? Call me what instrument you will, though you can fret me, you cannot play upon me.

Enter POLONIUS.

God bless you, sir.   360

POLONIUS My lord, the Queen would speak with you, and presently.

HAMLET Do you see yonder cloud that's almost in shape of a camel?

POLONIUS By th'Mass, and 'tis like a camel indeed.

HAMLET Methinks it is like a weasel.

POLONIUS It is backed like a weasel.

HAMLET Or like a whale?

POLONIUS Very like a whale.

HAMLET Then I will come to my mother by and by. [*Aside:*] They fool me to the top of my bent. – I will come by 370 and by.

POLONIUS I will say so.

                                     [*Exit Polonius.*

HAMLET   'By and by' is easily said. Leave me, friends.

                               [*Exeunt all but Hamlet.*

'Tis now the very witching time of night,
When churchyards yawn, and hell itself breathes out
Contagion to this world. Now could I drink hot blood,
And do such bitter business as the day
Would quake to look on. Soft, now to my mother.
O heart, lose not thy nature: let not ever
The soul of Nero enter this firm bosom;   380
Let me be cruel, not unnatural.
I will speak daggers to her, but use none.
My tongue and soul in this be hypocrites:
How in my words somever she be shent,
To give them seals never, my soul, consent!

                                        [*Exit.*

SCENE 3.

Enter KING, ROSENCRANTZ *and* GUILDENSTERN.

KING   I like him not, nor stands it safe with us
           To let his madness range. Therefore prepare you.
           I your commission will forthwith dispatch,
           And he to England shall along with you.
           The terms of our estate may not endure
           Hazard so near us as doth hourly grow
           Out of his brows.

GUILDEN.   We will ourselves provide.
           Most holy and religious fear it is
           To keep those many many bodies safe
           That live and feed upon your Majesty.   10

ROSENCR.   The single and peculiar life is bound
           With all the strength and armour of the mind
           To keep itself from noyance, but much more
           That spirit upon whose weal depends and rests
           The lives of many. The cess of majesty[89]
           Dies not alone, but like a gulf doth draw
           What's near it with it. Or 'tis a massy wheel
           Fixed on the summit of the highest mount,
           To whose huge spokes ten thousand lesser things
           Are mortised and adjoined; which when it falls,   20

Each small annexment, petty consequence,
Attends the boist'rous ruin. Never alone
Did the King sigh, but with a general groan.

KING   Arm you, I pray you, to this speedy voyage,
For we will fetters put about this fear,
Which now goes too free-footed.

ROSENCR.   We will haste us.

Exeunt Rosencrantz and Guildenstern. Enter POLONIUS.

POLONIUS   My lord, he's going to his mother's closet.
Behind the arras I'll convey myself
To hear the process. I'll warrant she'll tax him home,
And as you said, and wisely was it said,   30
'Tis meet that some more audience than a mother,
Since nature makes them partial, should o'erhear
The speech of vantage. Fare you well, my liege.
I'll call upon you ere you go to bed,
And tell you what I know.

KING   Thanks, dear my lord.
                               [*Exit Polonius.*

O, my offence is rank, it smells to heaven;
It hath the primal eldest curse[90] upon't –
A brother's murder. Pray can I not:
Though inclination be as sharp as will,
My stronger guilt defeats my strong intent,   40
And, like a man to double business bound,
I stand in pause where I shall first begin,
And both neglect. What if this cursèd hand
Were thicker than itself with brother's blood –
Is there not rain enough in the sweet heavens
To wash it white as snow? Whereto serves mercy
But to confront the visage of offence?
And what's in prayer but this twofold force,
To be forestallèd ere we come to fall,
Or pardoned being down? Then I'll look up.   50
My fault is past; but O, what form of prayer
Can serve my turn? 'Forgive me my foul murder'?
That cannot be, since I am still possessèd
Of those effects for which I did the murder:

My crown, mine own ambition, and my Queen.
May one be pardoned and retain th'offence?
In the corrupted currents of this world
Offence's gilded hand may shove by justice,
And oft 'tis seen the wicked prize itself
Buys out the law. But 'tis not so above: 60
There is no shuffling, there the action lies
In his true nature, and we ourselves compelled
Even to the teeth and forehead of our faults
To give in evidence. What then? What rests?
Try what repentance can. What can it not?
Yet what can it, when one can not repent?
O wretched state! O bosom black as death!
O limèd soul, that, struggling to be free,
Art more engaged! Help, angels: make assay.
Bow, stubborn knees; and heart, with strings of steel,   70
Be soft as sinews of the new-born babe.   [*He kneels.*
All may be well.

Enter HAMLET.

HAMLET   Now might I do it pat, now he is a-praying;
And now I'll do't; [*he draws his sword*] and so he
                                            goes to heaven,
And so am I revenged. That would be scanned:
A villain kills my father, and for that
I, his sole son, do this same villain send
To heaven.
Why, this is hire and salary, not revenge.[91]
He took my father grossly, full of bread,   80
With all his crimes broad blown, as flush as May;
And how his audit stands, who knows save heaven?
But in our circumstance and course of thought,
'Tis heavy with him. And am I then revenged,
To take him in the purging of his soul,
When he is fit and seasoned for his passage?
No.   [*He sheathes his sword:*
Up, sword, and know thou a more horrid hent:
When he is drunk asleep, or in his rage,
Or in th'incestuous pleasure of his bed,   90

At game, a-swearing, or about some act
That has no relish of salvation in't,
Then trip him, that his heels may kick at heaven,
And that his soul may be as damned and black
As hell, whereto it goes. My mother stays.
This physic but prolongs thy sickly days.   [*Exit.*

KING   [*rises.*] My words fly up, my thoughts remain below.
Words without thoughts never to heaven go.

                                           [*Exit.*

SCENE 4.

The Queen's closet hung with an arras.

Enter QUEEN *and* POLONIUS.

POLONIUS He will come straight. Look you lay home to him:
Tell him his pranks have been too broad to bear with,
And that your grace hath screened and stood between
Much heat and him. I'll silence me even here.
Pray you be round with him.

HAMLET [*outside:*] Mother, mother, mother!

QUEEN   I'll warrant you;
Fear me not. Withdraw, I hear him coming.

                        [*Polonius hides behind the arras.*

Enter HAMLET.

HAMLET Now, mother, what's the matter?

QUEEN Hamlet, thou hast thy father much offended.

HAMLET Mother, you have my father much offended.   10

QUEEN Come, come, you answer with an idle tongue.

HAMLET Go, go, you question with a wicked tongue.

QUEEN Why, how now, Hamlet?

HAMLET   What's the matter now?

QUEEN Have you forgot me?

HAMLET   No, by the rood, not so.
You are the Queen, your husband's brother's wife,
And, would it were not so, you are my mother.

QUEEN Nay then, I'll set those to you that can speak.

HAMLET   Come, come, and sit you down. You shall not budge.
          You go not till I set you up a glass
          Where you may see the inmost part of you.   20
QUEEN   What wilt thou do? Thou wilt not murder me?
          Help, help, ho!
POLONIUS [*behind the arras:*] What, ho! Help, help, help!
HAMLET   [*draws.*] How now! A rat? Dead, for a ducat, dead.
                        [*He thrusts his sword through the arras.*
POLONIUS [*falling:*] O, I am slain!
QUEEN   O me, what hast thou done?
HAMLET   Nay, I know not. Is it the King?
                        [*He lifts up the arras and discovers Polonius, dead.*
QUEEN   O what a rash and bloody deed is this!
HAMLET   A bloody deed. Almost as bad, good mother,
          As kill a king, and marry with his brother.
QUEEN   As kill a king!
HAMLET   Ay, lady, it was my word.
          [*To Polonius:*] Thou wretched, rash, intruding fool,
                                                farewell!   30
          I took thee for thy better. Take thy fortune:
          Thou find'st to be too busy is some danger.
          [*To Queen:*] Leave wringing of your hands. Peace,
                                                sit you down,
          And let me wring your heart: for so I shall,
          If it be made of penetrable stuff,
          If damnèd custom have not brassed it so
          That it be proof and bulwark against sense.
QUEEN   What have I done, that thou dar'st wag thy tongue
          In noise so rude against me?
HAMLET   Such an act
          That blurs the grace and blush of modesty,   40
          Calls virtue hypocrite, takes off the rose
          From the fair forehead of an innocent love
          And sets a blister there, makes marriage vows
          As false as dicers' oaths – O such a deed
          As from the body of contraction plucks
          The very soul, and sweet religion makes
          A rhapsody of words. Heaven's face does glow;
          Yea, this solidity and compound mass

With tristful visage, as against the doom,
Is thought-sick at the act.[92]

QUEEN
　　　　　　　　　　　　　　Ay me, what act,　　　50
That roars so loud, and thunders in the index?

HAMLET
Look here, upon this picture, and on this;
The counterfeit presentment of two brothers.
See what a grace was seated on this brow:
Hyperion's curls, the front of Jove himself,
An eye like Mars to threaten and command,
A station like the herald Mercury
New-lighted on a heaven-kissing hill,
A combination and a form indeed
Where every god did seem to set his seal　　　60
To give the world assurance of a man.
This was your husband. Look you now what follows.
Here is your husband, like a mildewed ear,
Blasting his wholesome brother. Have you eyes?
Could you on this fair mountain leave to feed,
And batten on this moor? Ha! Have you eyes?
You cannot call it love, for at your age
The heyday in the blood is tame, it's humble,
And waits upon the judgement; and what judgement
Would step from this to this? Sense sure you have,　　　70
Else could you not have motion, but sure that sense
Is apoplexed, for madness would not err,
Nor sense to ecstasy was ne'er so thralled,
But it reserved some quantity of choice
To serve in such a difference.[93] What devil was't
That thus hath cozened you at hoodman-blind?
Eyes without feeling, feeling without sight,
Ears without hands or eyes, smelling sans all,
Or but a sickly part of one true sense,
Could not so mope.[94] O shame, where is thy blush?　　　80
Rebellious hell,
If thou canst mutine in a matron's bones,
To flaming youth let virtue be as wax
And melt in her own fire; proclaim no shame
When the compulsive ardour gives the charge,
Since frost itself as actively doth burn,[95]

And reason pandars will.

QUEEN   O Hamlet, speak no more.
Thou turn'st my eyes into my very soul,
And there I see such black and grainèd spots
As will not leave their tinct.

HAMLET   Nay, but to live   90
In the rank sweat of an enseamèd bed,
Stewed in corruption, honeying and making love
Over the nasty sty —

QUEEN   O speak to me no more.
These words like daggers enter in mine ears.
No more, sweet Hamlet.

HAMLET   A murderer and a villain,
A slave that is not twentieth part the tithe
Of your precédent lord; a Vice of kings,
A cutpurse of the empire and the rule,
That from a shelf the precious diadem stole
And put it in his pocket —

QUEEN   No more.
HAMLET   A king   100
Of shreds and patches —

Enter the GHOST *in his night-gown.*

Save me and hover o'er me with your wings,
You heavenly guards! — What would your gracious
                                        figure?

QUEEN   Alas, he's mad.
HAMLET   Do you not come your tardy son to chide,
That, lapsed in time and passion, lets go by
Th'important acting of your dread command?
O, say!

GHOST   Do not forget! This visitation
Is but to whet thy almost blunted purpose.
But look, amazement on thy mother sits.   110
O step between her and her fighting soul;
Conceit in weakest bodies strongest works.
Speak to her, Hamlet.

HAMLET   How is't with you, lady?
QUEEN   Alas, how is't with *you,*

	That you do bend your eye on vacancy,	
	And with th'incorporal air do hold discourse?	
	Forth at your eyes your spirits wildly peep,	
	And, as the sleeping soldiers in th'alarm,	
	Your bedded hairs, like life in excrements,	
	Start up and stand on end.[96] O gentle son,	120
	Upon the heat and flame of thy distemper	
	Sprinkle cool patience. Whereon do you look?	
HAMLET	On him, on *him*! Look you how pale he glares.	
	His form and cause conjoined, preaching to stones,	
	Would make them capable. – Do not look upon me,	
	Lest with this piteous action you convert	
	My stern effects. Then what I have to do	
	Will want true colour – tears perchance for blood.	
QUEEN	To whom do you speak this?	
HAMLET	Do you see nothing there?	
QUEEN	Nothing at all, yet all that is I see.	130
HAMLET	Nor did you nothing hear?	
QUEEN	No, nothing but ourselves.	
HAMLET	Why, look you there: look how it steals away:	
	My father in his habit as he lived!	
	Look where he goes, even now, out at the portal.	

                                        [*Exit Ghost.*

QUEEN	This is the very coinage of your brain.	
	This bodiless creation ecstasy	
	Is very cunning in.[97]	
HAMLET	Ecstasy?	
	My pulse as yours doth temperately keep time,	
	And makes as healthful music. It is not madness	140
	That I have uttered. Bring me to the test,	
	And I the matter will re-word, which madness	
	Would gambol from. Mother, for love of grace,	
	Lay not that flattering unction to your soul,	
	That not your trespass but my madness speaks.	
	It will but skin and film the ulcerous place,	
	Whilst rank corruption, mining all within,	
	Infects unseen.[98] Confess yourself to heaven,	
	Repent what's past, avoid what is to come,	
	And do not spread the compost on the weeds	150

To make them ranker. Forgive me this my virtue,
For, in the fatness of these pursy times,
Virtue itself of vice must pardon beg;
Yea, curb and woo for leave to do him good.

QUEEN   O Hamlet, thou hast cleft my heart in twain.

HAMLET O throw away the worser part of it,
And live the purer with the other half.
Good night; but go not to my uncle's bed:
Assume a virtue if you have it not.
That monster custom, who all sense doth eat   160
Of habits evil, is angel yet in this,
That to the use of actions fair and good
He likewise gives a frock or livery
That aptly is put on.[99] Refrain tonight,
And that shall lend a kind of easiness
To the next abstinence, the next more easy:
For use almost can change the stamp of nature,
And either [house][100] the devil, or throw him out,
With wondrous potency. Once more, good night,
And when you are desirous to be blessed,   170
I'll blessing beg of you. For this same lord,
I do repent; but heaven hath pleased it so,
To punish me with this, and this with me,
That I must be their scourge and minister.
I will bestow him and will answer well
The death I gave him; so again, good night.
I must be cruel only to be kind.
Thus bad begins, and worse remains behind.
One word more, good lady.

QUEEN   What shall I do?

HAMLET Not this, by no means, that I bid you do: 180
Let the bloat King tempt you again to bed,
Pinch wanton on your cheek, call you his mouse,
And let him for a pair of reechy kisses,
Or paddling in your neck with his damned fingers,
Make you to ravel all this matter out,
That I essentially am not in madness,
But mad in craft. 'Twere good you let him know,
For who that's but a queen, fair, sober, wise,

Would from a paddock, from a bat, a gib,
Such dear concernings hide? Who would do so?   190
No, in despite of sense and secrecy,
Unpeg the basket on the house's top,
Let the birds fly, and, like the famous ape,
To try conclusions, in the basket creep,
And break your own neck down.[101]

QUEEN   Be thou assured, if words be made of breath,
And breath of life, I have no life to breathe
What thou hast said to me.

HAMLET   I must to England, you know that?

QUEEN   Alack,
I had forgot; 'tis so concluded on.   200

HAMLET   There's letters sealed, and my two school-fellows –
Whom I will trust as I will adders fanged –
They bear the mandate. They must sweep my way
And marshal me to knavery: let it work,
For 'tis the sport to have the engineer
Hoist with his own petar, and't shall go hard
But I will delve one yard below their mines,
And blow them at the moon. O, 'tis most sweet
When in one line two crafts directly meet.[102]
This man shall set me packing.   210
I'll lug the guts into the neighbour room.
Mother, good night indeed. This counsellor
Is now most still, most secret, and most grave,
Who was in life a foolish prating knave. –
Come, sir, to draw toward an end with you. –
Good night, mother.

                        [Exit Hamlet, tugging Polonius.

ACT 4, SCENE 1.[103]

QUEEN *remains. Enter* KING *with* ROSENCRANTZ
and GUILDENSTERN.

KING There's matter in these sighs, these prófound heaves.
   You must translate: 'tis fit we understand them.
   Where is your son?

QUEEN Bestow this place on us a little while.
         [*Exeunt Rosencrantz and Guildenstern.*
   Ah, mine own lord, what have I seen tonight!

KING What, Gertrude? How does Hamlet?

QUEEN Mad as the sea and wind when both contend
   Which is the mightier. In his lawless fit,
   Behind the arras hearing something stir,
   Whips out his rapier, cries 'A rat, a rat!'   10
   And in this brainish apprehension kills
   The unseen good old man.

KING   O heavy deed!
   It had been so with us had we been there.
   His liberty is full of threats to all,
   To you yourself, to us, to everyone.
   Alas, how shall this bloody deed be answered?
   It will be laid to us, whose providence
   Should have kept short, restrained and out of haunt
   This mad young man; but so much was our love,
   We would not understand what was most fit,   20
   But, like the owner of a foul disease,
   To keep it from divulging, let it feed
   Even on the pith of life. Where is he gone?

QUEEN To draw apart the body he hath killed,
   O'er whom – his very madness, like some ore
   Among a mineral of metals base,
   Shows itself pure – he weeps for what is done.

KING O Gertrude, come away.
   The sun no sooner shall the mountains touch,
   But we will ship him hence; and this vile deed   30
   We must with all our majesty and skill

Both countenance and excuse. Ho! Guildenstern!

Enter ROSENCRANTZ *and* GUILDENSTERN.

Friends both, go join you with some further aid.
Hamlet in madness hath Polonius slain,
And from his mother's closet hath he dragged him.
Go, seek him out, speak fair, and bring the body
Into the chapel; I pray you, haste in this.

      [Exeunt Rosencrantz and Guildenstern.

Come, Gertrude, we'll call up our wisest friends,
And let them know both what we mean to do
And what's untimely done. [So haply slander,] [104]   40
Whose whisper o'er the world's diameter,
As level as the cannon to his blank,
Transports his poisoned shot, may miss our name,
And hit the woundless air.[105] O come away!
My soul is full of discord and dismay.

            [Exeunt.

SCENE 2.

Another room of the castle.

Enter HAMLET.

HAMLET Safely stowed.

VOICES OUTSIDE Hamlet! Lord Hamlet!

HAMLET What noise? Who calls on Hamlet? O, here they come!

Enter ROSENCRANTZ, GUILDENSTERN *and* OTHERS.

ROSENCR. What have you done, my lord, with the dead body?

HAMLET Compounded it with dust, whereto 'tis kin.

ROSENCR. Tell us where 'tis, that we may take it thence,
    And bear it to the chapel.

HAMLET Do not believe it.

ROSENCR. Believe what?

HAMLET That I can keep your counsel and not mine own. 10
    Besides, to be demanded of a sponge – what replication
    should be made by the son of a king?

ROSENCR. Take you me for a sponge, my lord?

HAMLET   Ay, sir, that soaks up the King's countenance, his
          rewards, his authorities. But such officers do the King
          best service in the end: he keeps them, like an ape, in
          the corner of his jaw, first mouthed to be last swal-
          lowed.[106] When he needs what you have gleaned, it is
          but squeezing you, and, sponge, you shall be dry again.

ROSENCR. I understand you not, my lord.   20

HAMLET   I am glad of it. A knavish speech sleeps in a foolish ear.

ROSENCR. My lord, you must tell us where the body is, and go
          with us to the King.

HAMLET   The body is with the King, but the King is not with
          the body. The King is a thing –

GUILDEN. A thing, my lord?

HAMLET   Of nothing, bring me to him. Hide fox, and all after!
                                                              [Exeunt.

SCENE 3.

The hall of the castle.

Enter KING *with two or three* LORDS.

KING   I have sent to seek him, and to find the body.
          How dangerous is it that this man goes loose!
          Yet must not we put the strong law on him:
          He's loved of the distracted multitude,
          Who like not in their judgement but their eyes,[107]
          And where 'tis so, th'offender's scourge is weighed
          But never the offence. To bear all smooth and even,
          This sudden sending him away must seem
          Deliberate pause.[108] Diseases desperate grown
          By desperate appliance are relieved,   10
          Or not at all.

                    Enter ROSENCRANTZ *and* ATTENDANTS.

                              How now? What hath befall'n?

ROSENCR. Where the dead body is bestowed, my lord,
          We cannot get from him.

KING   But where is he?

ROSENCR.	Without, my lord, guarded, to know your pleasure.
KING	Bring him before us.
ROSENCR.	Ho! Bring in the lord.

Enter HAMLET *and* GUILDENSTERN.

KING	Now, Hamlet, where's Polonius?
HAMLET	At supper.
KING	At supper? Where?
HAMLET	Not where he eats, but where he is eaten. A certain convocation of politic worms are e'en at him. Your worm 20 is your only emperor for diet: we fat all creatures else to fat us, and we fat ourselves for maggots. Your fat king and your lean beggar is but variable service, two dishes, but to one table. That's the end.
KING	Alas, alas!
HAMLET	A man may fish with the worm that hath eat of a king, and eat of the fish that hath fed of that worm.[109]
KING	What dost thou mean by this?
HAMLET	Nothing but to show you how a king may go a progress through the guts of a beggar. 30
KING	Where is Polonius?
HAMLET	In heaven: send thither to see. If your messenger find him not there, seek him i'th'other place yourself. But if indeed you find him not within this month, you shall nose him as you go up the stairs into the lobby.
KING	[*to attendants:*] Go seek him there.
HAMLET	He will stay till you come. [*Exeunt attendants.*
KING	Hamlet, this deed, for thine especial safety (Which we do tender, as we dearly grieve For that which thou hast done), must send thee hence 40 With fiery quickness. Therefore prepare thyself. The bark is ready, and the wind at help, Th'associates tend, and everything is bent For England.
HAMLET	For England?
KING	Ay, Hamlet.
HAMLET	Good.
KING	So is it, if thou knew'st our purposes.
HAMLET	I see a cherub[110] that sees them. But, come, for England!

| | Farewell, dear mother. | 50 |

KING   Thy loving father, Hamlet.

HAMLET   My mother. Father and mother is man and wife, man
and wife is one flesh,[111] and so my mother. Come, for
England!   [*Exit.*

KING   [*to Rosencrantz and Guildenstern:*]
Follow him at foot, tempt him with speed aboard,
Delay it not: I'll have him hence tonight.
Away, for everything is sealed and done
That else leans on th'affair. Pray you, make haste.
                            [*Exeunt all but the King.*
And, England, if my love thou hold'st at aught –
As my great power thereof may give thee sense,   60
Since yet thy cicatrice looks raw and red
After the Danish sword, and thy free awe
Pays homage to us – thou mayst not coldly set
Our sovereign process, which imports at full,
By letters congruing to that effect,
The present death of Hamlet. Do it, England,
For like the hectic in my blood he rages,
And thou must cure me. Till I know 'tis done,
Howe'er my haps, my joys were ne'er begun.
                                   [*Exit.*

SCENE 4.

Open ground.

Enter FORTINBRAS, *his* CAPTAIN,
and other SOLDIERS *of his army.*[112]

FORTIN.   Go, captain, from me greet the Danish King.
Tell him that by his licence, Fortinbras
Craves the conveyance of a promised march
Over his kingdom. You know the rendezvous.
If that his Majesty would aught with us,
We shall express our duty in his eye,
And let him know so.

CAPTAIN   I will do't, my lord.

FORTIN.   [to the other soldiers:] Go softly on.
                              [Exeunt Fortinbras and the other soldiers.
                    Enter HAMLET, ROSENCRANTZ,
                      GUILDENSTERN and OTHERS.

HAMLET   [to Captain:] Good sir, whose powers are these?
CAPTAIN   They are of Norway, sir.   10
HAMLET   How purposed, sir, I pray you?
CAPTAIN   Against some part of Poland.
HAMLET   Who commands them, sir?
CAPTAIN   The nephew to old Norway, Fortinbras.
HAMLET   Goes it against the main of Poland, sir,
               Or for some frontier?
CAPTAIN   Truly to speak, and with no addition,
               We go to gain a little patch of ground
               That hath in it no profit but the name.
               To pay five ducats, five, I would not farm it;   20
               Nor will it yield to Norway or the Pole
               A ranker rate should it be sold in fee.
HAMLET   Why, then the Polack never will defend it.
CAPTAIN   Yes, it is already garrisoned.
HAMLET   Two thousand souls and twenty thousand ducats
               Will not debate the question of this straw!
               This is th'imposthume of much wealth and peace,
               That inward breaks, and shows no cause without
               Why the man dies. I humbly thank you, sir.
CAPTAIN   God buy you, sir.   [Exit.
ROSENCR.   Will't please you go, my lord?   30
HAMLET   I'll be with you straight; go a little before.
                                          [Exeunt all but Hamlet.
               How all occasions do inform against me,
               And spur my dull revenge! What is a man,
               If his chief good and market of his time
               Be but to sleep and feed? A beast, no more:
               Sure he that made us with such large discourse,
               Looking before and after, gave us not
               That capability and god-like reason
               To fust in us unused. Now, whether it be
               Bestial oblivion, or some craven scruple   40

Of thinking too precisely on th'event
(A thought which, quartered, hath but one part wisdom,
And ever three parts coward), I do not know
Why yet I live to say 'This thing's to do',
Sith I have cause, and will, and strength, and means,
To do't. Examples gross as earth exhort me.
Witness this army of such mass and charge,
Led by a delicate and tender prince,
Whose spirit with divine ambition puffed
Makes mouths at the invisible event,   50
Exposing what is mortal and unsure
To all that fortune, death and danger dare,
Even for an egg-shell. Rightly to be great
Is not to stir without great argument,[113]
But greatly to find quarrel in a straw
When honour's at the stake. How stand I then,
That have a father killed, a mother stained,
Excitements of my reason and my blood,
And let all sleep, while to my shame I see
The imminent death of twenty thousand men,   60
That for a fantasy and trick of fame
Go to their graves like beds, fight for a plot
Whereon the numbers cannot try the cause,
Which is not tomb enough and continent
To hide the slain? O, from this time forth,
My thoughts be bloody, or be nothing worth![114]

                                                        [*Exit.*

SCENE 5.

A room in the castle of Elsinore.

Enter QUEEN, HORATIO *and a* GENTLEMAN.

QUEEN   I will not speak with her.
GENT.   She is importunate, indeed distract.
          Her mood will needs be pitied.
QUEEN   What would she have?
GENT.   She speaks much of her father, says she hears
          There's tricks i'th'world, and hems, and beats her heart,

Spurns enviously at straws, speaks things in doubt
That carry but half sense. Her speech is nothing,
Yet the unshapèd use of it doth move
The hearers to collection: they aim at it,
And botch the words up fit to their own thoughts,   10
Which, as her winks and nods and gestures yield them,
Indeed would make one think there might be thought,
Though nothing sure, yet much unhappily.

HORATIO   'Twere good she were spoken with, for she may strew
Dangerous conjectures in ill-breeding minds.

QUEEN   Let her come in.   [*Exit Gentleman.*
[*Aside:*] To my sick soul, as sin's true nature is,
Each toy seems prologue to some great amiss.
So full of artless jealousy is guilt,
It spills itself, in fearing to be spilt.[115]   20

Enter OPHELIA.

OPHELIA   Where is the beauteous Majesty of Denmark?

QUEEN   How now, Ophelia?

OPHELIA   [*sings:*] How should I your true love know
               From another one?
                  By his cockle hat and staff,
                  And his sandal shoon.[116]

QUEEN   Alas, sweet lady, what imports this song?

OPHELIA   Say you? Nay, pray you mark.
[*Sings:*] He is dead and gone, lady,
               He is dead and gone;   30
                 At his head a grass-green turf,
                 At his heels a stone.
O ho!

QUEEN   Nay, but Ophelia –

OPHELIA   Pray you mark.
[*Sings:*] White his shroud as the mountain snow –

Enter KING.

QUEEN   Alas, look here, my lord.

OPHELIA   [*sings:*] Larded all with sweet flowers,
               Which bewept to the grave did not go
               With true-love showers.

KING   How do you, pretty lady?

OPHELIA   Well, God 'ild you! They say the owl was a baker's 40
           daughter.[117] Lord, we know what we are, but know
           not what we may be. God be at your table!

KING   Conceit upon her father.

OPHELIA   Pray you let's have no words of this, but when they ask
           you what it means, say you this:
           [sings:] 'Tomorrow is Saint Valentine's day,
                       All in the morning betime,
                   And I a maid at your window,
                       To be your Valentine.'[118]
                   Then up he rose, and donned his clo'es, 50
                       And dupped the chamber door;
                   Let in the maid, that out a maid
                       Never departed more.

KING   Pretty Ophelia!

OPHELIA   Indeed, la, without an oath, I'll make an end on't –
           [sings:] By Gis and by Saint Charity,
                       Alack and fie for shame!
                   Young men will do't, if they come to't:
                       By Cock, they are to blame.
                   Quoth she, 'Before you tumbled me, 60
                       You promised me to wed.'
           He answers,
                   'So would I ha' done, by yonder sun,
                       An thou hadst not come to my bed.'

KING   How long hath she been thus?

OPHELIA   I hope all will be well. We must be patient, but I
           cannot choose but weep to think they would lay him
           i'th'cold ground. My brother shall know of it. And so I
           thank you for your good counsel. Come, my coach!
           Good night, ladies, good night. Sweet ladies, good 70
           night, good night.   [Exit.

KING   Follow her close, give her good watch, I pray you.
                                                    [Exit Horatio.

           O, this is the poison of deep grief: it springs
           All from her father's death – and now behold!
           O Gertrude, Gertrude,
           When sorrows come, they come not single spies,
           But in battalions: first her father slain;

Next, your son gone, and he most violent author
Of his own just remove; the people muddied,
Thick and unwholesome in their thoughts and whispers 80
For good Polonius' death – and we have done but
                                                greenly,
In hugger-mugger to inter him; poor Ophelia
Divided from herself and her fair judgement,
Without the which we are pictures or mere beasts;
Last, and as much containing as all these,
Her brother is in secret come from France,
Feeds on his wonder, keeps himself in clouds,[119]
And wants not buzzers to infect his ear
With pestilent speeches of his father's death,
Wherein necessity, of matter beggared,   90
Will nothing stick our person to arraign
In ear and ear.[120] O my dear Gertrude, this,
Like to a murdering-piece, in many places
Gives me superfluous death.   [*A tumult outside.*

QUEEN   Alack! what noise is this?
KING   [*calls:*] Attend!

                    Enter ATTENDANT.

Where are my Switzers? Let them guard the door.
What is the matter?
ATTENDANT   Save yourself, my lord!
The ocean, overpeering of his list,
Eats not the flats with more impetuous haste   100
Than young Laertes, in a riotous head,
O'erbears your officers: the rabble call him lord,
And as the world were now but to begin,
Antiquity forgot, custom not known
(The ratifiers and props of every word),
They cry 'Choose we, Laertes shall be King!'
Caps, hands and tongues applaud it to the clouds,
'Laertes shall be King, Laertes King!'
                              [*Louder tumult outside.*

QUEEN   How cheerfully on the false trail they cry!
          O, this is counter, you false Danish dogs!   110
KING   The doors are broke.

Enter LAERTES, *armed, and several* DANES.

LAERTES   Where is this king? Sirs, stand you all without.
DANES   No, let's come in.
LAERTES   I pray you, give me leave.
DANES   We will, we will.
LAERTES   I thank you, keep the door.   [*Exeunt Danes.*
                              O thou vile king,
          Give me my father.
QUEEN   Calmly, good Laertes.
LAERTES   That drop of blood that's calm proclaims me bastard,
          Cries cuckold to my father, brands the harlot,
          Even here, between the chaste unsmirchèd brows
          Of my true mother.
KING   What is the cause, Laertes,   120
          That thy rebellion looks so giant-like? –
          Let him go, Gertrude; do not fear our person.
          There's such divinity doth hedge a king
          That treason can but peep to what it would,
          Acts little of his will. – Tell me, Laertes,
          Why thou art thus incensed. – Let him go, Gertrude.
          – Speak, man.
LAERTES   Where is my father?
KING   Dead.
QUEEN   But not by him.
KING   Let him demand his fill.
LAERTES   How came he dead? I'll not be juggled with.   130
          To hell allegiance! Vows to the blackest devil!
          Conscience and grace to the profoundest pit!
          I dare damnation. To this point I stand,
          That both the worlds I give to negligence,
          Let come what comes; only I'll be revenged
          Most throughly for my father.[121]
KING   Who shall stay you?
LAERTES   My will, not all the world's;
          And for my means, I'll husband them so well,
          They shall go far with little.
KING   Good Laertes,
          If you desire to know the certainty   140

Of your dear father's death, is't writ in your revenge
That, swoopstake, you will draw both friend and foe,
Winner and loser?[122]

LAERTES   None but his enemies.

KING   Will you know them then?

LAERTES   To his good friends thus wide I'll ope my arms,
And, like the kind life-rend'ring pelican,
Repast them with my blood.[123]

KING   Why, now you speak
Like a good child and a true gentleman.
That I am guiltless of your father's death,
And am most sensibly in grief for it,   150
It shall as level to your judgment 'pear,
As day does to your eye.

VOICES OUTSIDE   Let her come in.

LAERTES   How now! What noise is that?

        Enter OPHELIA, *holding flowers.*

O heat, dry up my brains, tears seven times salt
Burn out the sense and virtue of mine eye!
By heaven, thy madness shall be paid with weight,
Till our scale turn the beam. O rose of May,
Dear maid, kind sister, sweet Ophelia!
O heavens, is't possible a young maid's wits
Should be as mortal as an old man's life?   160
Nature is fine in love, and where 'tis fine,
It sends some precious instance of itself
After the thing it loves.[124]

OPHELIA   [*sings:*] They bore him barefaced on the bier,
              Hey non nonny, nonny, hey nonny,
           And in his grave rained many a tear –
             Fare you well, my dove!

LAERTES   Hadst thou thy wits, and didst persuade revenge,
It could not move thus.

OPHELIA   You must sing 'Adown adown', and you 'Call him   170
adown-a'. O, how the wheel becomes it![125] It is the
false steward that stole his master's daughter.

LAERTES   This nothing's more than matter.[126]

OPHELIA   [*to Laertes:*] There's rosemary, that's for remembrance –

	pray you, love, remember – and there is pansies, that's for thoughts.[127]
LAERTES	A document in madness: thoughts and remembrance fitted.
OPHELIA	[to the King:] There's fennel for you, and columbines. [To the Queen:] There's rue for you,[128] and here's some 180 for me; we may call it herb of grace o' Sundays. O, you must wear your rue with a difference. There's a daisy. I would give you some violets, but they withered all, when my father died. They say he made a good end. [Sings:] For bonny sweet Robin is all my joy –
LAERTES	Thought and affliction, passion, hell itself, She turns to favour and to prettiness.
OPHELIA	[sings:] And will he not come again? And will he not come again? No, no, he is dead; 190 Go to thy death-bed; He never will come again.
	His beard was as white as snow; All flaxen was his poll. He is gone, he is gone, And we cast away moan; God ha' mercy on his soul! – And of all Christian souls I pray God. God buy you. [Exit.
LAERTES	Do you see this, O God?
KING	Laertes, I must cómmune with your grief, 200 Or you deny me right. Go but apart, Make choice of whom your wisest friends you will, And they shall hear and judge 'twixt you and me. If by direct or by collateral hand They find us touched, we will our kingdom give, Our crown, our life, and all that we call ours, To you in satisfaction; but if not, Be you content to lend your patience to us, And we shall jointly labour with your soul To give it due content.
LAERTES	Let this be so. 210

His means of death, his óbscure funeral
(No trophy, sword, nor hatchment o'er his bones,
No noble rite, nor formal ostentation),
Cry to be heard as 'twere from heaven to earth,
That I must call't in question.

KING　　　　　　　　　　　　　　　So you shall,
And where th'offence is, let the great axe fall.
I pray you, go with me.

　　　　　　　　　　　　　　　　　　　　[Exeunt.

SCENE 6.[129]

Enter HORATIO *and a* SERVANT.

HORATIO　What are they that would speak with me?
SERVANT　Sailors, sir. They say they have letters for you.
HORATIO　Let them come in.　　　　　　　*[Exit Servant.*
　　　　　I do not know from what part of the world
　　　　　I should be greeted, if not from Lord Hamlet.

Enter SAILORS.

SAILOR I　God bless you, sir.
HORATIO　Let him bless thee too.
SAILOR I　He shall, sir, an't please him. There's a letter for you,
　　　　　sir – it came from th'ambassador that was bound for
　　　　　England – if your name be Horatio, as I am let to know　10
　　　　　it is.
HORATIO　[*reads:*] 'Horatio, when thou shalt have overlooked this,
　　　　　give these fellows some means to the King: they have
　　　　　letters for him. Ere we were two days old at sea, a pirate
　　　　　of very warlike appointment gave us chase. Finding
　　　　　ourselves too slow of sail, we put on a compelled valour.
　　　　　In the grapple, I boarded them. On the instant they got
　　　　　clear of our ship, so I alone became their prisoner. They
　　　　　have dealt with me like thieves of mercy, but they knew
　　　　　what they did; I am to do a good turn for them. Let the　20
　　　　　King have the letters I have sent, and repair thou to me
　　　　　with as much speed as thou wouldest fly death. I have
　　　　　words to speak in thine ear will make thee dumb, yet are

they much too light for the bore of the matter. These
good fellows will bring thee where I am. Rosencrantz
and Guildenstern hold their course for England; of them
I have much to tell thee. Farewell.

             He that thou knowest thine, Hamlet.'
Come, I will give you way for these your letters,
And do't the speedier that you may direct me   30
To him from whom you brought them.

                                  [*Exeunt.*

SCENE 7.

Enter KING *and* LAERTES.

KING   Now must your conscience my acquittance seal,
And you must put me in your heart for friend,
Sith you have heard, and with a knowing ear,
That he which hath your noble father slain
Pursued my life.

LAERTES   It well appears; but tell me
Why you proceeded not against these feats,
So crimeful and so capital in nature,
As by your safety, greatness, wisdom, all things else,
You mainly were stirred up.

KING   O, for two special reasons,
Which may to you perhaps seem much unsinewed,   10
But yet to me they're strong. The Queen his mother
Lives almost by his looks, and for myself –
My virtue or my plague, be it either which –
She's so conjunctive to my life and soul
That, as the star moves not but in his sphere,
I could not but by her. The other motive,
Why to a public count I might not go,
Is the great love the general gender bear him,
Who, dipping all his faults in their affection,
Would, like the spring that turneth wood to stone,[130]   20
Convert his gyves to graces; so that my arrows,
Too slightly timbered for so loud a wind,
Would have reverted to my bow again,

And not where I had aimed them.

LAERTES   And so have I a noble father lost,
A sister driven into desp'rate terms,
Whose worth, if praises may go back again,
Stood challenger on mount of all the age
For her perfections. But my revenge will come.

KING   Break not your sleeps for that. You must not think   30
That we are made of stuff so flat and dull
That we can let our beard be shook with danger
And think it pastime. You shortly shall hear more.
I loved your father, and we love ourself,
And that, I hope, will teach you to imagine –

      Enter a MESSENGER *with letters.*

How now! What news?

MESSENGER   Letters, my lord, from Hamlet.
These to your Majesty, this to the Queen.

KING   From Hamlet? Who brought them?

MESSENGER Sailors, my lord, they say. I saw them not.
They were given me by Claudio; he received them   40
Of him that brought them.

KING   Laertes, you shall hear them.
[*To Messenger:*] Leave us.   [*Exit Messenger.*
[*He reads:*] 'High and mighty, you shall know I am set
naked on your kingdom. Tomorrow shall I beg leave
to see your kingly eyes, when I shall, first asking your
pardon, thereunto recount the occasion of my sudden
and more strange return.   Hamlet.'
What should this mean? Are all the rest come back?
Or is it some abuse, and no such thing?

LAERTES   Know you the hand?

KING   'Tis Hamlet's character. 'Naked' 50
– And in a postscript here he says 'alone'.
Can you advise me?

LAERTES   I am lost in it, my lord; but let him come!
It warms the very sickness in my heart
That I shall live and tell him to his teeth
'Thus diest thou.'[131]

KING   If it be so, Laertes, –

As how should it be so? How otherwise? –
Will you be ruled by me?

LAERTES   Ay, my lord,
So you will not o'errule me to a peace.

KING   To thine own peace. If he be now returned,   60
As checking at his voyage, and that he means
No more to undertake it, I will work him
To an exploit, now ripe in my device,
Under the which he shall not choose but fall;
And for his death no wind of blame shall breathe,
But even his mother shall uncharge the practice
And call it accident.

LAERTES   My lord, I will be ruled,
The rather if you could devise it so
That I might be the organ.

KING   It falls right.
You have been talked of since your travel much,   70
And that in Hamlet's hearing, for a quality
Wherein they say you shine. Your sum of parts
Did not together pluck such envy from him
As did that one, and that in my regard
Of the unworthiest siege.

LAERTES   What part is that, my lord?

KING   A very riband in the cap of youth,
Yet needful too, for youth no less becomes
The light and careless livery that it wears,
Than settled age his sables and his weeds
Importing health and graveness.[132] Two months since, 80
Here was a gentleman of Normandy –
I have seen myself, and served against, the French,
And they can well on horseback – but this gallant
Had witchcraft in't, he grew unto his seat,
And to such wondrous doing brought his horse
As had he been incorpsed and demi-natured
With the brave beast.[133] So far he topped my thought,
That I in forgery of shapes and tricks[134]
Come short of what he did.

LAERTES   A Norman was't?

KING	A Norman.	90
LAERTES	Upon my life, Lamord.[135]	
KING	The very same.	
LAERTES	I know him well: he is the brooch indeed	
	And gem of all the nation.	
KING	He made confession of you,	

And gave you such a masterly report
For art and exercise in your defence,
And for your rapier most especially,
That he cried out 'twould be a sight indeed
If one could match you; the scrimers of their nation
He swore had neither motion, guard, nor eye,   100
If you opposed them.[136] Sir, this report of his
Did Hamlet so envenom with his envy,
That he could nothing do but wish and beg
Your sudden coming o'er to play with him.
Now, out of this . . .

LAERTES   What out of this, my lord?

KING   Laertes, was your father dear to you?
Or are you like the painting of a sorrow,
A face without a heart?

LAERTES   Why ask you this?

KING   Not that I think you did not love your father,
But that I know love is begun by time,   110
And that I see, in passages of proof,
Time qualifies the spark and fire of it.
There lives within the very flame of love
A kind of wick or snuff that will abate it,
And nothing is at a like goodness still,
For goodness, growing to a pleurisy,
Dies in his own too much.[137] That we would do
We should do when we would: for this 'would'
                                 changes,
And hath abatements and delays as many
As there are tongues, are hands, are accidents;   120
And then this 'should' is like a spendthrift sigh,
That hurts by easing. But, to the quick o'th'ulcer: [138]
Hamlet comes back; what would you undertake
To show yourself your father's son in deed

More than in words?

LAERTES   To cut his throat i'th'church.

KING No place indeed should murder sanctuarize:
Revenge should have no bounds. But, good Laertes,
Will you do this, keep close within your chamber;
Hamlet returned shall know you are come home;
We'll put on those shall praise your excellence   130
And set a double varnish on the fame
The Frenchman gave you, bring you in fine together,
And wager on your heads. He, being remiss,
Most generous, and free from all contriving,
Will not peruse the foils, so that with ease,
Or with a little shuffling, you may choose
A sword unbated, and in a pass of practice
Requite him for your father.

LAERTES   I will do't;
And, for the purpose, I'll anoint my sword.
I bought an unction of a mountebank,   140
So mortal, that but dip a knife in it,
Where it draws blood, no cataplasm so rare,
Collected from all simples that have virtue
Under the moon, can save the thing from death
That is but scratched withal. I'll touch my point
With this contagion, that if I gall him slightly,
It may be death.[139]

KING   Let's further think of this;
Weigh what convenience both of time and means
May fit us to our shape. If this should fail,
And that our drift look through our bad performance, 150
'Twere better not essayed. Therefore this project
Should have a back or second that might hold,
If this did blast in proof; soft, let me see,
We'll make a solemn wager on your cunnings –
I ha't!
When in your motion you are hot and dry –
As make your bouts more violent to that end –
And that he calls for drink, I'll have prepared him
A chalice for the nonce, whereon but sipping,
If he by chance escape your venomed stuck,   160

Our purpose may hold there. But stay, what noise?

Enter QUEEN.

QUEEN One woe doth tread upon another's heel,
So fast they follow. Your sister's drowned, Laertes.

LAERTES Drowned! O where?

QUEEN There is a willow grows aslant a brook,
That shows his hoar leaves in the glassy stream.
Therewith fantastic garlands did she make
Of crow-flowers, nettles, daisies, and long purples
That liberal shepherds give a grosser name,[140]
But our cold maids do 'Dead Men's Fingers' call them. 170
There on the pendent boughs her crownet weeds[141]
Clamb'ring to hang, an envious sliver broke,
When down her weedy trophies and herself
Fell in the weeping brook. Her clothes spread wide,
And mermaid-like awhile they bore her up,
Which time she chanted snatches of old tunes,
As one incapable of her own distress,
Or like a creature native and indued
Unto that element; but long it could not be
Till that her garments, heavy with their drink,   180
Pulled the poor wretch from her melodious lay
To muddy death.

LAERTES   Alas, then she is drowned.

QUEEN Drowned, drowned.

LAERTES Too much of water hast thou, poor Ophelia,
And therefore I forbid my tears; but yet
It is our trick, nature her custom holds,
Let shame say what it will. When these are gone,
The woman will be out.[142] Adieu, my lord!
I have a speech o' fire that fain would blaze,
But that this folly douts it.   [*Exit*.

KING   Let's follow, Gertrude.   190
How much I had to do to calm his rage!
Now fear I, this will give it start again;
Therefore let's follow.

                                                [*Exeunt*.

ACT 5, SCENE I.

A grave-yard, with a newly opened grave.

Enter two CLOWNS *(a grave-digger and his companion).*

CLOWN 1   Is she to be buried in Christian burial, when she
          wilfully seeks her own salvation? [143]

CLOWN 2   I tell thee she is, therefore make her grave straight.
          The crowner hath sat on her, and finds it Christian
          burial. [144]

CLOWN 1   How can that be, unless she drowned herself in her
          own defence?

CLOWN 2   Why, 'tis found so.

CLOWN 1   It must be 'se offendendo', [145] it cannot be else. For here
          lies the point: if I drown myself wittingly, it argues an   10
          act; and an act hath three branches: it is to act, to do, and
          to perform. Argal, she drowned herself wittingly.

CLOWN 2   Nay, but hear you, goodman delver — [146]

CLOWN 1   Give me leave. Here lies the water — good. Here stands
          the man — good. If the man go to this water and drown
          himself, it is, will he nill he, he goes, mark you that.
          But if the water come to him, and drown him, he
          drowns not himself. Argal, he that is not guilty of his
          own death, shortens not his own life.

CLOWN 2   But is this law?   20

CLOWN 1   Ay, marry is't: crowner's quest law. [147]

CLOWN 2   Will you ha' the truth on't? If this had not been a
          gentlewoman, she should have been buried out of
          Christian burial.

CLOWN 1   Why, there thou say'st; and the more pity that great
          folk should have countenance in this world to drown
          or hang themselves more than their even-Christian.
          Come, my spade! There is no ancient gentlemen but
          gardeners, ditchers and grave-makers: they hold up
          Adam's profession.   30
                               [*He goes down into the open grave.*

CLOWN 2   Was he a gentleman?

CLOWN 1	A was the first that ever bore arms.[148]
CLOWN 2	Why, he had none.
CLOWN 1	What, art a heathen? How dost thou understand the Scripture? The Scripture says Adam digged; could he dig without arms? I'll put another question to thee. If thou answerest me not to the purpose, confess thyself –
CLOWN 2	Go to.[149]
CLOWN 1	What is he that builds stronger than either the mason, the shipwright, or the carpenter?
CLOWN 2	The gallows-maker, for that frame outlives a thousand tenants.
CLOWN 1	I like thy wit well in good faith, the gallows does well – but how does it well? It does well to those that do ill. Now thou dost ill to say the gallows is built stronger than the church; argal, the gallows may do well to thee. To't again, come.
CLOWN 2	Who builds stronger than a mason, a shipwright, or a carpenter?
CLOWN 1	Ay, tell me that, and unyoke.
CLOWN 2	Marry, now I can tell.
CLOWN 1	To't.
CLOWN 2	Mass, I cannot tell.
CLOWN 1	Cudgel thy brains no more about it, for your dull ass will not mend his pace with beating; and when you are asked this question next, say 'a grave-maker'. The houses he makes lasts till doomsday. Go, get thee to Yaughan,[150] and fetch me a stoup of liquor.

> *[Exit Second Clown.*

> *Enter* HAMLET *and* HORATIO.
> *First Clown digs and sings:*

> In youth when I did love, did love,
>   Methought it was very sweet,
> To contract O the time for a[151] my behove,
>   O, methought there was nothing meet.[152]

HAMLET	Has this fellow no feeling of his business, that he sings in grave-making?
HORATIO	Custom hath made it in him a property of easiness.

Line numbers in margin: 40, 50, 60

HAMLET   'Tis e'en so, the hand of little employment hath the
            daintier sense.

CLOWN I   [sings:] But age with his stealing steps
                        Hath clawed me in his clutch,
                        And hath shipped me intil the land,[153]   70
                        As if I had never been such.
                                            [He throws out a skull.

HAMLET   That skull had a tongue in it, and could sing once.
            How the knave jowls it to the ground, as if 'twere
            Cain's jaw-bone, that did the first murder! This might
            be the pate of a politician, which this ass now o'er-
            reaches;[154] one that would circumvent God, might it
            not?

HORATIO   It might, my lord.

HAMLET   Or of a courtier, which could say 'Good morrow,
            sweet lord! How dost thou, good lord?' This might be   80
            my Lord Such-a-one, that praised my Lord Such-a-
            one's horse, when he meant to beg it, might it not?

HORATIO   Ay, my lord.

HAMLET   Why, e'en so; and now my Lady Worm's, chopless and
            knocked about the mazard with a sexton's spade;
            here's fine revolution, if we had the trick to see't! Did
            these bones cost no more the breeding, but to play at
            loggats with them?[155] Mine ache to think on't.

CLOWN I   [sings:] A pick-axe and a spade, a spade,
                        For and a shrouding-sheet;   90
                        O, a pit of clay for to be made
                        For such a guest is meet.
                                            [He throws out a second skull.

HAMLET   There's another. Why, may not that be the skull of a
            lawyer? Where be his quiddities now, his quillities, his
            cases, his tenures, and his tricks? Why does he suffer
            this rude knave now to knock him about the sconce
            with a dirty shovel, and will not tell him of his action
            of battery?[156] Hum! This fellow might be in's time a
            great buyer of land, with his statutes, his recognizances,
            his fines, his double vouchers, his recoveries. Is this the   100
            fine of his fines, and the recovery of his recoveries, to
            have his fine pate full of fine dirt? Will his vouchers

vouch him no more of his purchases, and double
ones too, than the length and breadth of a pair of
indentures? The very conveyances of his lands will
scarcely lie in this box, and must th'inheritor himself
have no more, ha?

HORATIO   Not a jot more, my lord.

HAMLET   Is not parchment made of sheep-skins?

HORATIO   Ay, my lord, and of calves'-skins too.   110

HAMLET   They are sheep and calves which seek out assurance in
that. I will speak to this fellow. – Whose grave's this,
sirrah?

CLOWN I   Mine, sir. [*He sings:*]
> O, a pit of clay for to be made
> For such a guest is meet.

HAMLET   I think it be thine indeed, for thou liest in't.

CLOWN I   You lie out on't, sir, and therefore 'tis not yours; for
my part I do not lie in't, and yet it is mine.

HAMLET   Thou dost lie in't, to be in't and say it is thine. 'Tis for   120
the dead, not for the quick – therefore thou liest.

CLOWN I   'Tis a quick lie, sir, 'twill away again from me to you.

HAMLET   What man dost thou dig it for?

CLOWN I   For no man, sir.

HAMLET   What woman then?

CLOWN I   For none neither.

HAMLET   Who is to be buried in't?

CLOWN I   One that was a woman, sir, but – rest her soul – she's dead.

HAMLET   How absolute the knave is! We must speak by the card,
or equivocation will undo us. By the Lord, Horatio, –   130
these three years I have taken note of it – the age is
grown so picked, that the toe of the peasant comes so
near the heel of the courtier he galls his kibe. – How
long hast thou been grave-maker?

CLOWN I   Of all the days i'th'year, I came to't that day that our
last King Hamlet overcame Fortinbras.

HAMLET   How long is that since?

CLOWN I   Cannot you tell that? Every fool can tell that. It was
that very day that young Hamlet was born: he that is
mad and sent into England.   140

HAMLET   Ay, marry; why was he sent into England?

CLOWN I   Why, because a was mad: a shall recover his wits there,
           or if a do not, 'tis no great matter there.

HAMLET   Why?

CLOWN I   'Twill not be seen in him there: there the men are as
           mad as he.

HAMLET   How came he mad?

CLOWN I   Very strangely, they say.

HAMLET   How strangely?

CLOWN I   Faith, e'en with losing his wits.   150

HAMLET   Upon what ground?

CLOWN I   Why, here in Denmark. I have been sexton here, man
           and boy, thirty years.

HAMLET   How long will a man lie i'th'earth ere he rot?

CLOWN I   Faith, if a be not rotten before a die (as we have many
           pocky corses nowadays that will scarce hold the laying
           in), a will last you some eight year or nine year. A
           tanner will last you nine year.

HAMLET   Why he, more than another?

CLOWN I   Why sir, his hide is so tanned with his trade, that a will   160
           keep out water a great while; and your water is a sore
           decayer of your whoreson dead body. Here's a skull
           now: this skull hath lien you i'th'earth three-and-
           twenty years.

HAMLET   Whose was it?

CLOWN I   A whoreson mad fellow's it was. Whose do you think
           it was?

HAMLET   Nay, I know not.

CLOWN I   A pestilence on him for a mad rogue! A poured a
           flagon of Rhenish on my head once. This same skull,   170
           sir, was, sir, Yorick's skull, the King's jester.

HAMLET   This?

CLOWN I   E'en that.

HAMLET   Let me see. [*He takes the skull.*] Alas, poor Yorick! I
           knew him, Horatio: a fellow of infinite jest, of most
           excellent fancy. He hath borne me on his back a thou-
           sand times; and now how abhorred in my imagination
           it is! My gorge rises at it. Here hung those lips that I
           have kissed I know not how oft. Where be your
           gibes now? Your gambols, your songs, your flashes of   180

merriment that were wont to set the table on a roar? Not one now to mock your own grinning? Quite chop-fallen? Now get you to my lady's chamber, and tell her, let her paint an inch thick, to this favour she must come.[157] Make her laugh at that. Prithee, Horatio, tell me one thing.

HORATIO   What's that, my lord?

HAMLET   Dost thou think Alexander looked o' this fashion i'th' earth?

HORATIO   E'en so.   190

HAMLET   And smelt so? Pah!   [*He throws down the skull.*

HORATIO   E'en so, my lord.

HAMLET   To what base uses we may return, Horatio! Why may not imagination trace the noble dust of Alexander,[158] till he find it stopping a bung-hole?

HORATIO   'Twere to consider too curiously, to consider so.

HAMLET   No, faith, not a jot; but to follow him thither with modesty enough, and likelihood to lead it; as thus: Alexander died, Alexander was buried, Alexander returneth to dust, the dust is earth, of earth we make 200 loam, and why of that loam whereto he was converted might they not stop a beer-barrel?

        Imperious Caesar,[159] dead and turned to clay,
        Might stop a hole to keep the wind away.
        O, that that earth, which kept the world in awe,
        Should patch a wall t'expel the winter's flaw!
        But soft, but soft awhile: here comes the King,
        The Queen, the courtiers.

Hamlet and Horatio stand aside as a procession enters the grave-yard:
BEARERS *with the corpse of* OPHELIA *in an open coffin, followed by*
a PRIEST, LAERTES, *the* KING, *the* QUEEN *and* COURTIERS.

                            Who is this they follow,
        And with such maimèd rites? This doth betoken
        The corse they follow did with desperate hand   210
        Fordo its own life. 'Twas of some estate.
        Couch we awhile, and mark.

LAERTES   What ceremony else?

HAMLET   That is Laertes,

A very noble youth. Mark.

LAERTES   What ceremony else?

PRIEST   Her obsequies have been as far enlarged
As we have warranty. Her death was doubtful,
And but that great command o'ersways the order,
She should in ground unsanctified have lodged
Till the last trumpet;[160] for charitable prayers,   220
Shards, flints and pebbles should be thrown on her.
Yet here she is allowed her virgin crants,
Her maiden strewments, and the bringing home
Of bell and burial.

LAERTES   Must there no more be done?

PRIEST   No more be done!
We should profane the service of the dead
To sing sage requiem and such rest to her
As to peace-parted souls.

LAERTES   Lay her i'th'earth,
And from her fair and unpolluted flesh
May violets spring![161] [The coffin is laid within the grave.]
                    I tell thee, churlish priest,   230
A minist'ring angel shall my sister be,
When thou liest howling.

HAMLET   What, the fair Ophelia!

QUEEN   [scattering flowers:] Sweets to the sweet. Farewell!
I hoped thou shouldst have been my Hamlet's wife:
I thought thy bride-bed to have decked, sweet maid,
And not have strewed thy grave.

LAERTES   O, treble woe
Fall ten times treble on that cursèd head
Whose wicked deed thy most ingenious sense
Deprived thee of! Hold off the earth awhile,
Till I have caught her once more in mine arms;   240
                    [He leaps into the grave.
Now pile your dust upon the quick and dead,
Till of this flat a mountain you have made
T'o'ertop old Pelion or the skyish head
Of blue Olympus.[162]

HAMLET   [coming forward:]   What is he whose grief
Bears such an emphasis, whose phrase of sorrow

	Conjures the wand'ring stars and makes them stand
	Like wonder-wounded hearers?[163] This is I,
	Hamlet the Dane.[164] *[He leaps in after Laertes.*
LAERTES	*[grappling with him:]* The devil take thy soul!
HAMLET	Thou pray'st not well.
	I prithee take thy fingers from my throat; 250
	For though I am not splenative and rash,
	Yet have I in me something dangerous,
	Which let thy wiseness fear. Hold off thy hand.
KING	Pluck them asunder.
QUEEN	Hamlet, Hamlet!
ALL	Gentlemen!
HORATIO	Good my lord, be quiet.

*[Courtiers part them, and they
come up out of the grave.*

HAMLET	Why, I will fight with him upon this theme
	Until my eyelids will no longer wag.
QUEEN	O my son, what theme?
HAMLET	I loved Ophelia. Forty thousand brothers
	Could not with all their quantity of love 260
	Make up my sum. What wilt thou do for her?
KING	O, he is mad, Laertes.
QUEEN	For love of God, forbear him.
HAMLET	'Swounds, show me what thou't do:
	Woo't weep? Woo't fight? Woo't fast? Woo't
	tear thyself?
	Woo't drink up eisel? Eat a crocodile?
	I'll do't. Dost thou come here to whine?
	To outface me with leaping in her grave?
	Be buried quick with her, and so will I.
	And if thou prate of mountains, let them throw 270
	Millions of acres on us, till our ground,
	Singeing his pate against the burning zone,
	Make Ossa like a wart![165] Nay, an thou'lt mouth,
	I'll rant as well as thou.
QUEEN	This is mere madness,
	And thus awhile the fit will work on him.
	Anon, as patient as the female dove
	When that her golden couplets are disclosed,

His silence will sit drooping.

HAMLET   Hear you, sir,
What is the reason that you use me thus?
I loved you ever. But it is no matter: 280
Let Hercules himself do what he may,
The cat will mew, and dog will have his day.[166] [Exit.

KING   I pray thee, good Horatio, wait upon him.
                                                    [Exit Horatio.
[Aside to Laertes:] Strengthen your patience in
                                    our last night's speech:
We'll put the matter to the present push. –
Good Gertrude, set some watch over your son. –
This grave shall have a living monument;[167]
An hour of quiet shortly shall we see,
Till then, in patience our proceeding be.

                                                        [Exeunt.

SCENE 2.

The hall of the castle.

Enter HAMLET *and* HORATIO.

HAMLET   So much for this, sir; now shall you see the other.
You do remember all the circumstance?

HORATIO   Remember it, my lord!

HAMLET   Sir, in my heart there was a kind of fighting
That would not let me sleep. Methought I lay
Worse than the mutines in the bilboes. Rashly –
And praised be rashness for it: let us know
Our indiscretion sometime serves us well
When our deep plots do pall, and that should learn us
There's a divinity that shapes our ends,   10
Rough-hew them how we will –

HORATIO   That is most certain.

HAMLET   Up from my cabin,
My sea-gown scarfed about me, in the dark
Groped I to find out them, had my desire,
Fingered their packet, and in fine withdrew

	To mine own room again, making so bold	
	(My fears forgetting manners) to unseal	
	Their grand commission; where I found, Horatio –	
	Ah, royal knavery! – an exact command,	
	Larded with many several sorts of reasons,	20
	Importing Denmark's health and England's too,	
	With, ho, such bugs and goblins in my life,	
	That on the supervise, no leisure bated,	
	No, not to stay the grinding of the axe,	
	My head should be struck off.	

HORATIO   Is't possible?

HAMLET   Here's the commission, read it at more leisure.
But wilt thou hear now how I did proceed?

HORATIO   I beseech you.

HAMLET   Being thus be-netted round with villainies –
Ere I could make a prologue to my brains,   30
They had begun the play – I sat me down,
Devised a new commission, wrote it fair –
I once did hold it, as our statists do,
A baseness to write fair, and laboured much
How to forget that learning, but, sir, now
It did me yeoman's service.[168] Wilt thou know
Th'effect of what I wrote?

HORATIO   Ay, good my lord.

HAMLET   An earnest conjuration from the King,
As England was his faithful tributary,
As love between them like the palm might flourish,   40
As peace should still her wheaten garland wear [169]
And stand a commere[170] 'tween their amities,
And many such like ases[171] of great charge,
That on the view and knowing of these contents
Without debatement further more or less,
He should those bearers put to sudden death,
Not shriving-time allowed.

HORATIO   How was this sealed?

HAMLET   Why, even in that was heaven ordinant.
I had my father's signet in my purse,
Which was the model of that Danish seal;   50
Folded the writ up in the form of th'other,

Subscribed it, gave't th'impression, placed it safely,
The changeling never known. Now, the next day
Was our sea-fight, and what to this was sequent
Thou knowest already.

HORATIO   So Guildenstern and Rosencrantz go to't.

HAMLET   Why, man, they did make love to this employment.[172]
They are not near my conscience; their defeat
Does by their own insinuation grow.
'Tis dangerous when the baser nature comes   60
Between the pass and fell incensèd points
Of mighty opposites.

HORATIO   Why, what a king is this!

HAMLET   Does it not, think thee, stand me now upon –
He that hath killed my king, and whored my mother,
Popped in between th'election and my hopes,
Thrown out his angle for my proper life,
And with such cozenage – is't not perfect conscience
To quit him with this arm? And is't not to be damned,
To let this canker of our nature come
In further evil?[173]   70

HORATIO   It must be shortly known to him from England
What is the issue of the business there.

HAMLET   It will be short. The interim is mine,
And a man's life's no more than to say 'one'.[174]
But I am very sorry, good Horatio,
That to Laertes I forgot myself;
For by the image of my cause I see
The portraiture of his. I'll court his favours;
But sure the bravery of his grief did put me
Into a towering passion.

HORATIO   Peace, who comes here?[175]   80

Enter OSRIC, *a young courtier, taking off his hat.*

OSRIC   Your lordship is right welcome back to Denmark.

HAMLET   I humbly thank you, sir. [*Aside:*] Dost know this water-fly?

HORATIO   No, my good lord.

HAMLET   Thy state is the more gracious, for 'tis a vice to know
him. He hath much land, and fertile. Let a beast be lord of
beasts, and his crib shall stand at the King's mess.[176] 'Tis

a chough, but, as I say, spacious in the possession of dirt.

OSRIC   Sweet lord, if your lordship were at leisure, I should impart a thing to you from his Majesty.

HAMLET   I will receive it, sir, with all diligence of spirit. Put your 90 bonnet to his right use: 'tis for the head.

OSRIC   I thank your lordship, it is very hot.

HAMLET   No, believe me, 'tis very cold, the wind is northerly.

OSRIC   It is indifferent cold, my lord, indeed.

HAMLET   But yet, methinks, it is very sultry and hot for my complexion.

OSRIC   Exceedingly, my lord, it is very sultry – as 'twere – I cannot tell how. But, my lord, his Majesty bade me signify to you that he has laid a great wager on your head. Sir, this is the matter, – 100

HAMLET   [*again urging him to put on his hat:*] I beseech you remember –

OSRIC   Nay, good my lord, for mine ease, in good faith. Sir, here is newly come to court Laertes; believe me, an absolute gentleman, full of most excellent differences, of very soft society, and great showing: indeed, to speak feelingly of him, he is the card or calendar of gentry; for you shall find in him the continent of what parts a gentleman would see.

HAMLET   Sir, his definement suffers no perdition in you, though I know to divide him inventorially would dizzy[177] 110 th'arithmetic of memory, and yet but yaw neither in respect of his quick sail; but in the verity of extolment I take him to be a soul of great article, and his infusion of such dearth and rareness as, to make true diction of him, his semblable is his mirror, and who else would trace him? His umbrage, nothing more.

OSRIC   Your lordship speaks most infallibly of him.

HAMLET   The concernancy, sir? Why do we wrap the gentleman in our more rawer breath?

OSRIC   Sir? 120

HORATIO   Is't not possible to understand in another tongue? You will to't, sir, really.

HAMLET   What imports the nomination of this gentleman?

OSRIC   Of Laertes?

HORATIO   [*aside to Hamlet:*] His purse is empty already, all's golden
            words are spent.

HAMLET   Of him, sir.

OSRIC   I know you are not ignorant –

HAMLET   I would you did, sir, yet in faith if you did, it would
            not much approve me. Well, sir?[178]   130

OSRIC   You are not ignorant of what excellence Laertes is –

HAMLET   I dare not confess that, lest I should compare with him
            in excellence, but to know a man well were to know
            himself.

OSRIC   I mean, sir, for his weapon; but in the imputation laid
            on him by them in his meed, he's unfellowed.[179]

HAMLET   What's his weapon?

OSRIC   Rapier and dagger.

HAMLET   That's two of his weapons; but well.

OSRIC   The King, sir, hath wagered with him six Barbary   140
            horses, against the which he has impawned, as I take it,
            six French rapiers and poniards, with their assigns, as
            girdle, hangers, and so. Three of the carriages, in faith,
            are very dear to fancy, very responsive to the hilts,
            most delicate carriages, and of very liberal conceit.

HAMLET   What call you 'the carriages'?

HORATIO   [*aside to Hamlet:*] I knew you must be edified by the
            margent ere you had done.

OSRIC   The carriages, sir, are the hangers.

HAMLET   The phrase would be more germane to the matter, if   150
            we could carry a cannon by our sides – I would it might
            be hangers till then. But on! Six Barbary horses against
            six French swords, their assigns, and three liberal-
            conceited carriages – that's the French bet against the
            Danish. Why is this all 'impawned', as you call it?

OSRIC   The King, sir, hath laid, sir, that in a dozen passes
            between yourself and him, he shall not exceed you
            three hits. He hath laid on twelve for nine.[180] And it
            would come to immediate trial, if your lordship would
            vouchsafe the answer.   160

HAMLET   How if I answer 'no'?

OSRIC   I mean, my lord, the opposition of your person in trial.

HAMLET   Sir, I will walk here in the hall, if it please his Majesty.

It is the breathing time of day with me. Let the foils be
brought, the gentleman willing, and the King hold his
purpose, I will win for him an I can; if not, I will gain
nothing but my shame and the odd hits.

OSRIC   Shall I re-deliver you e'en so?

HAMLET   To this effect, sir, after what flourish your nature will.

OSRIC   I commend my duty to your lordship.   170

HAMLET   Yours, yours.   [Exit Osric.
          He does well to commend it himself, there are no
          tongues else for's turn.

HORATIO   This lapwing runs away with the shell on his head.[181]

HAMLET   He did comply with his dug before he sucked it.[182]
          Thus has he – and many more of the same bevy that I
          know the drossy age dotes on – only got the tune of the
          time and, out of an habit of encounter, a kind of yeasty
          collection,[183] which carries them through and through
          the most fanned and winnowed opinions;[184] and do but   180
          blow them to their trial, the bubbles are out.

                          Enter a LORD.

LORD   My lord, his Majesty commended him to you by young
          Osric, who brings back to him that you attend him in
          the hall. He sends to know if your pleasure hold to play
          with Laertes, or that you will take longer time.

HAMLET   I am constant to my purposes, they follow the King's
          pleasure. If his fitness speaks, mine is ready, now or
          whensoever, provided I be so able as now.

LORD   The King and Queen and all are coming down.

HAMLET   In happy time.   190

LORD   The Queen desires you to use some gentle entertainment
          to Laertes before you fall to play.

HAMLET   She well instructs me.   [Exit Lord.[185]

HORATIO   You will lose this wager, my lord.

HAMLET   I do not think so. Since he went into France, I have
          been in continual practice. I shall win at the odds; but
          thou wouldst not think how ill all's here about my
          heart – but it is no matter.

HORATIO   Nay, good my lord –

HAMLET   It is but foolery, but it is such a kind of gain-giving as 200
          would perhaps trouble a woman.

HORATIO   If your mind dislike anything, obey it. I will forestall
            their repair hither, and say you are not fit.

HAMLET   Not a whit; we defy augury. There is special provid-
            ence in the fall of a sparrow.[186] If it be now, 'tis not to
            come; if it be not to come, it will be now; if it be not
            now, yet it will come: the readiness is all. Since no
            man, of aught he leaves, knows: what is't to leave
            betimes? Let be.[187]

Enter ATTENDANTS *to set a table and seating;* TRUMPETERS
and DRUMMERS; *the* KING, *the* QUEEN, LAERTES, OSRIC,
            COURTIERS, *and* ATTENDANTS *with foils.*

KING   Come, Hamlet, come and take this hand from me.   210
                 [*He puts the hand of Laertes into the hand of Hamlet.*

HAMLET   [*to Laertes:*] Give me your pardon, sir. I've done
                                                    you wrong:
            But pardon't, as you are a gentleman.
            This presence knows, and you must needs have heard,
            How I am punished with a sore distraction.
            What I have done
            That might your nature, honour and exception
            Roughly awake, I here proclaim was madness.
            Was't Hamlet wronged Laertes? Never Hamlet.
            If Hamlet from himself be ta'en away,
            And when he's not himself does wrong Laertes,   220
            Then Hamlet does it not; Hamlet denies it.
            Who does it then? His madness. If't be so,
            Hamlet is of the faction that is wronged:
            His madness is poor Hamlet's enemy.
            Sir, in this audience,
            Let my disclaiming from a purposed evil
            Free me so far in your most generous thoughts,
            That I have shot my arrow o'er the house,
            And hurt my brother.[188]

LAERTES   I am satisfied in nature,
            Whose motive in this case should stir me most   230
            To my revenge, but in my terms of honour
            I stand aloof, and will no reconcilement,
            Till by some elder masters of known honour

I have a voice and precedent of peace,
To keep my name ungored;[189] but till that time,
I do receive your offered love like love,
And will not wrong it.

HAMLET   I embrace it freely,
And will this brother's wager frankly play.
Give us the foils: come on.

LAERTES   Come, one for me.

HAMLET   I'll be your foil, Laertes. In mine ignorance   240
Your skill shall like a star i'th'darkest night
Stick fiery off indeed.

LAERTES   You mock me, sir.

HAMLET   No, by this hand.

KING   Give them the foils, young Osric.
                              [*Osric brings forward some foils.*
                                              Cousin Hamlet,
You know the wager?

HAMLET   Very well, my lord.
Your Grace has laid the odds o'th'weaker side.

KING   I do not fear it. I have seen you both.
But since he is bettered, we have therefore odds.

LAERTES   [*comparing foils:*] This is too heavy: let me see another.

HAMLET   [*taking a foil from Osric:*]
This likes me well. These foils have all a length?   250

OSRIC   Ay, my good lord.

           While Hamlet and Laertes prepare to fence,
                attendants fetch stoups of wine.

KING   Set me the stoups of wine upon that table.
If Hamlet give the first or second hit,
Or quit in answer of the third exchange,
Let all the battlements their ordnance fire.
The King shall drink to Hamlet's better breath,
And in the cup an union shall he throw,
Richer than that which four successive kings
In Denmark's crown have worn. Give me the cups,
And let the kettle to the trumpet speak,   260
The trumpet to the cannoneer without,
The cannons to the heavens, the heaven to earth,

'Now the King drinks to Hamlet.' Come, begin,
And you, the judges, bear a wary eye.

                        [Trumpets sound.

HAMLET   Come on, sir.

LAERTES   Come, my lord.

                              [They fence.

HAMLET   One!

LAERTES   No.

HAMLET   Judgement?

OSRIC   A hit, a very palpable hit.   270

          [They break off; the kettle-drum and trumpets sound,
                           and a cannon-shot is heard.

LAERTES   Well, again.

KING   Stay, give me drink. Hamlet, this pearl is thine.
Here's to thy health!   *[He drinks, and then drops*
                           the pearl into a cup.
Give him the cup.

HAMLET   I'll play this bout first; set it by a while.
                     [An attendant sets it on a table.
Come.   *[They fence again.*
Another hit! What say you?

LAERTES   A touch, a touch, I do confess't.   *[They rest.*

KING   Our son shall win.

QUEEN   He's fat, and scant of breath.
Here, Hamlet, take my napkin, rub thy brows.   280
      [She gives it him, and takes up his cup of wine.
The Queen carouses to thy fortune, Hamlet.

HAMLET   Good madam.

KING   Gertrude, do not drink.

QUEEN   I will, my lord; I pray you pardon me.
          [She drinks, and offers the cup to Hamlet.

KING   *[aside:]* It is the poisoned cup — it is too late!

HAMLET   I dare not drink yet, madam; by and by.

QUEEN   Come, let me wipe thy face.   *[She does so.*

LAERTES   *[to the King:]* My lord, I'll hit him now.

KING   I do not think't.

LAERTES   And yet 'tis almost 'gainst my conscience.

HAMLET   Come, for the third, Laertes. You do but dally;   290
I pray you pass with your best violence.

| | I am afeard you make a wanton of me. |
| LAERTES | Say you so? Come on. |

[The third bout ensues.

OSRIC	Nothing neither way.
LAERTES	Have at you now! *[Laertes wounds Hamlet, and in*
	scuffling they exchange rapiers.
KING	Part them: they are incensed.
HAMLET	Nay, come again. *[The Queen falls.*
OSRIC	Look to the Queen there, ho!

[Hamlet wounds Laertes.

| HORATIO | They bleed on both sides! How is it, my lord? |

[Laertes falls.

OSRIC	How is't, Laertes?
LAERTES	Why, as a woodcock to mine own springe, Osric. 300
	I am justly killed with mine own treachery.
HAMLET	How does the Queen?
KING	She swoons to see them bleed.
QUEEN	No, no, the drink, the drink! O my dear Hamlet!
	The drink, the drink! I am poisoned! *[She dies.*
HAMLET	O villainy! How? Let the door be locked. *[Exit Osric.*
	Treachery! Seek it out.
LAERTES	It is here, Hamlet. Hamlet, thou art slain.
	No med'cine in the world can do thee good:
	In thee there is not half an hour of life.
	The treacherous instrument is in thy hand, 310
	Unbated and envenomed. The foul practice
	Hath turned itself on me. Lo, here I lie,
	Never to rise again. Thy mother's poisoned.
	I can no more; the King, the King's to blame.
HAMLET	The point envenomed too! Then, venom, to thy work.

[He wounds the King.

ALL	Treason! Treason!
KING	O, yet defend me, friends: I am but hurt.
HAMLET	Here, thou incestuous, murderous, damnèd Dane,

[Hamlet forces him to drink.

	Drink off this potion: is thy union here?
	Follow my mother. *[The King dies.*
LAERTES	He is justly served: 320
	It is a poison tempered by himself.

Exchange forgiveness with me, noble Hamlet:
Mine and my father's death come not upon thee,
Nor thine on me.   [*He dies.*

HAMLET   Heaven make thee free of it! I follow thee.
I am dead, Horatio. Wretched Queen, adieu!
You that look pale and tremble at this chance,
That are but mutes or audience to this act,
Had I but time (as this fell sergeant, Death,
Is strict in his arrest), O, I could tell you –   330
But let it be. Horatio, I am dead;
Thou liv'st: report me and my cause aright
To the unsatisfied.

HORATIO   Never believe it;
I am more an antique Roman than a Dane:[190]
Here's yet some liquor left.   [*He takes the cup.*

HAMLET   As thou'rt a man,
Give me the cup. Let go, by heaven I'll ha't!
O God, Horatio, what a wounded name,
Things standing thus unknown, shall live behind me!
If thou didst ever hold me in thy heart,
Absent thee from felicity awhile,   340
And in this harsh world draw thy breath in pain
To tell my story.
     [*Offstage, sounds of marching troops and a volley of shots.*

                    Enter OSRIC.

                    What warlike noise is this?

OSRIC   Young Fortinbras, with conquest come from Poland,
To the ambassadors of England gives
This warlike volley.

HAMLET   O, I die, Horatio.
The potent poison quite o'er-crows my spirit.
I cannot live to hear the news from England;
But I do prophesy th'election lights
On Fortinbras. He has my dying voice.
So tell him, with th'occurrents more and less   350
Which have solicited – the rest is silence.   [*He dies.*

HORATIO   Now cracks a noble heart. Good night, sweet prince,
And flights of angels sing thee to thy rest.
Why does the drum come hither?

Enter FORTINBRAS, *the English* AMBASSADORS, *and* SOLDIERS.

FORTIN.   Where is this sight?

HORATIO   What is it you would see?
            If aught of woe or wonder, cease your search.

FORTIN.   This quarry cries on havoc. O proud Death,
            What feast is toward in thine eternal cell,
            That thou so many princes at a shot
            So bloodily hast struck?

AMBASS. I   The sight is dismal,   360
            And our affairs from England come too late.
            The ears are senseless that should give us hearing,
            To tell him his commandment is fulfilled,
            That Rosencrantz and Guildenstern are dead.
            Where should we have our thanks?

HORATIO   Not from his mouth,
            Had it th'ability of life to thank you.
            He never gave commandment for their death.
            But since, so jump upon this bloody question,
            You from the Polack wars, and you from England,
            Are here arrived, give order that these bodies   370
            High on a stage be placèd to the view,
            And let me speak to th'yet unknowing world
            How these things came about. So shall you hear
            Of carnal, bloody and unnatural acts,
            Of accidental judgments, casual slaughters,
            Of deaths put on by cunning and forced cause,
            And, in this upshot, purposes mistook
            Fall'n on th'inventors' heads: all this can I
            Truly deliver.

FORTIN.   Let us haste to hear it,
            And call the noblest to the audience.   380
            For me, with sorrow I embrace my fortune.
            I have some rights of memory in this kingdom,
            Which now to claim my vantage doth invite me.[191]

HORATIO   Of that I shall have also cause to speak,
            And from his mouth whose voice will draw on more.[192]
            But let this same be presently performed,
            Even while men's minds are wild, lest more mischance

On plots and errors happen.[193]

FORTIN.   Let four captains
Bear Hamlet like a soldier to the stage,
For he was likely, had he been put on,   390
To have proved most royally; and, for his passage,
The soldiers' music and the rite of war
Speak loudly for him.
Take up the bodies. Such a sight as this
Becomes the field, but here shows much amiss.[194]
Go, bid the soldiers shoot.

Exeunt, the soldiers marching as they carry the bodies;
after which a peal of ordnance is heard.

NOTES ON *HAMLET*

In these notes, the following abbreviations are used:

Cf., cf.:   *confer* (Latin): compare.

    F1:   First Folio (1623).

  i.e.:   *id est* (Latin): that is.

Jenkins: *Hamlet*, ed. Harold Jenkins (London and New York: Methuen, 1982).

Kittredge: *Hamlet*, ed. G. L. Kittredge (Boston: Ginn, 1939).

O.E.D.:   *The Oxford English Dictionary* (2nd edn.: Oxford: Oxford University Press, 1989).

    Q1:   First Quarto (1603).

    Q2:   Second Quarto (1604–5).

    Q3:   Third Quarto (1611).

  S.D.:   stage-direction.

Biblical quotations are from the Geneva Bible.

Where a pun or an ambiguity is glossed, the meanings are distinguished as (a) and (b). Where contrasting interpretations are possible, the alternatives are distinguished as (i) and (ii).

1 (1.1.15) *the Dane:* the King of Denmark. At line 61, 'Norway' means 'the King of Norway'.

2 (1.1.63) *He smote the sledded Polacks:* The First and Second Quartos (Q1 and Q2) have the phrase 'sleaded pollax'; the First Folio (F1) has 'sledded Pollax'. Some editors infer that the King smote *Polacks* (Polish warriors on sledges) during a battle; others infer that he thumped his *pole-axe* (halberd) on the ice during an angry dispute (though 'sleaded' is then obscure, perhaps a corruption of 'leaded', meaning 'weighted with lead').

3 (1.1.67–9) *In what . . . state:* 'I don't know what particular interpretation to pursue, but my general notion is that this event portends some unusual violent outbreak in the state.'

4 (1.1.93) *cov'nant:* Q2 has 'comart'; F1 has 'Cou'nant'. Some editors prefer the former, interpreting it as 'joint bargain', to the latter, meaning 'pact'.

5 (1.1.113–16) *In the most . . . streets:* Shakespeare, embellishing an account by Plutarch, had specified various supernatural portents in his *Julius Caesar*, Act 1, scene 3, and Act 2, scene 2.

6 (1.1.117–18) *Asters . . . sun:* Q2 gives: 'As starres with traines of fier, and dewes of blood / Disasters in the sunne'. Q1 and F1 have no equivalent. Many editors have proposed emendations. I adopt J. M. Glauser's phrasing here. 'Aster' meant 'heavenly body, e.g. star or planet'; 'asters with trains of fire' would be comets; and 'disastering' could then mean 'ill-starring' or 'blighting'.

7 (1.1.108–25) *I think it be . . . countrymen:* These lines are present in Q2 but absent from Q1 and F1.

8 (1.1.127) *S.D.:* Q2 has the ambiguous direction, '*It spreads his armes.*'. Some editors think this means that Horatio spreads his arms ('*It*' being an error for '*He*'), while others infer that the Ghost does so ('*his*' being equivalent to '*its*'). The gesture is appropriate for Horatio, who is attempting to halt the Ghost.

9 (1.2.65) *A little . . . kind:* 'A little closer than a mere kinsman, as you are my mother's husband, but hardly bearing a familial likeness to you (and not kindly disposed towards you).'

10 (1.2.67) *too much in the sun:* 'too close to the sunshine of royal favour, and too much a son' (as he is both King Hamlet's son and King Claudius's step-son).

11 (1.2.129) *too too solid flesh:* Q1 has 'too much grieu'd and sallied flesh'; Q2 has 'too too sallied flesh'; and F1 has 'too too solid Flesh'. Some editors prefer 'sallied', treating it as a version of 'sullied'; others prefer 'solid', which neatly anticipates 'melt'.

12 (1.2.131–2) *Or that . . . self-slaughter:* God's sixth commandment, 'Thou shalt not kill' (Exodus 20:13), was deemed to forbid suicide.

13 (1.2.157) *incestuous sheets:* Gertrude has married her brother-in-law; and, according to the canonical law of both the Roman

Catholic and the Protestant Churches (influenced by Leviticus 18:16 and 20:21), such marriages were incestuous and prohibited.

14 (1.3.36–7) *The chariest . . . moon:* 'The most prudent virgin would be acting rashly if she were to let even the moon, symbol of chastity, see her naked beauty'.

15 (1.3.44) *Youth . . . near:* 'a young person, even if alone, rebels against sexual restraints and experiences lust'.

16 (1.3.65) *comrade:* Q1 and Q2 have 'courage'; F1 has 'Comrade'. Some editors prefer the former, usually taking it to mean 'brave or swaggering person'.

17 (1.3.74) *Are . . . that:* 'are most discriminating and liberal, especially in that respect'. Q1 has 'Are of a most select and generall chiefe in that:'; Q2 has 'Or of a most select and generous, chiefe in that:'; and F1 has 'Are of a most select and generous cheffe in that.'.

18 (1.3.109) *Running it thus:* Q2 has 'Wrong it thus'; F1 has 'Roaming it thus'. The emendation 'Running it thus' is appropriate to the metaphor of broken-winded horse.

19 (1.3.120) *You . . . time:* Q2, which seems one syllable short, has 'You must not take for fire, from this time'; F1, which seems one syllable too long, has 'You must not take for fire. For this time Daughter'. The Q2 line becomes regular if 'fire' be pronounced disyllabically: '*fi*-er'.

20 (1.3.130) *Breathing . . . bonds:* 'sounding like sacred vows (of espousal)'. Some editors emend 'bonds' to 'bawds'.

21 (1.4.8–9) *The King . . . reels:* Editors' interpretations vary between (i): 'The King stays up tonight and carouses, joins in toast-drinking, and riotously performs the upspring [a dance or dance-step]'; and (ii): 'The King stays up tonight and carouses, participating in the drinking of toasts and in the ostentatious newfangled revels.'

22 (1.4.16) *observance:* The following lines 17–38 (from 'This heavy-headed revel' to 'scandal.') are found in Q2 but not in Q1 or F1.

23 (1.4.36–8) *The dram . . . scandal:* The word 'evil' is an editorial emendation of the Second Quarto's 'eale'. The sense then (though still strained) seems to be: 'The little drop of evil calls

into question the entire noble nature and thus brings it into disrepute.' Some editors emend 'eale' to 'ill' and 'of a doubt' to 'often dout' (meaning 'often douse or extinguish'). Other suggestions are that 'eale' and 'of a doubt' may be corruptions of 'niel' (black inlay used by engravers of silver) and 'overdight' (darken over).

24 (1.4.46) *rest in ignorance:* The early texts have 'burst in ignorance', but this probably results from an anticipation of the 'burst' in line 48.

25 (1.4.49) *interred:* Q1 and Q2 have 'interr'd'. F1 has 'enurn'd' (which some editors prefer, rendering it as 'inurned', i.e. 'entombed').

26 (1.4.75–8) *The very place . . . beneath:* These lines are present in Q2 but absent from Q1 and F1.

27 (1.5.11) *confined to fast in fires:* Some editors emend this as 'confinèd fast in fires'.

28 (1.5.21) *But things . . . be:* This is J. M. Glauser's emendation of a line which Q2 gives as 'But this eternall blazon must not be'. 'To blazon' is to proclaim or display.

29 (1.5.33) *That . . . wharf:* 'which rots away lethargically on the bank of the Lethe, the underworld river of forgetfulness'. Q1 and Q2 have 'rootes'; F1 has 'rots'. Some editors prefer to read 'roots'; but 'rots' fits the play's imagery of disease and decay, and brings to mind the 'lilies that fester' of Sonnet 94.

30 (1.5.63) *And in . . . pour:* The Duke of Urbino was murdered in 1538 – allegedly by poison dropped into his ears.

31 (1.5.116) *Come, bird, come:* originally the cry of a falconer recalling his hawk.

32 (1.5.136) *Saint Patrick:* This saint was sometimes deemed the keeper of Purgatory.

33 (1.5.154) *[They swear.:* The stage-direction '*They swear*' does not appear at any point in Q1, Q2 or F1. This edition, like some others, thrice inserts such a direction, so that the group swears secrecy here (concerning what was seen), at line 160 (concerning what was heard), and at line 181 (concerning Hamlet's behaviour). An alternative view is that Hamlet formulates a triple oath which the group, in spite of its endeavours, is not able to swear formally

and fully until line 181: a culmination which prompts Hamlet's words of reassurance, 'Rest, rest, perturbèd spirit!'. Previously (according to that reading), the endeavour to swear has been protracted as the Ghost has moved from one subterranean location to another. Stage-productions treat this business diversely, sometimes truncating it.

34 (1.5.166) *in your philosophy:* (a) in philosophical and scientific thought in general; (b) in Horatio's stoical philosophical outlook. (Q1 and Q2 have 'in your philosophie'. F1 has 'in our Philosophy'.)

35 (2.1.28) *season . . . charge:* 'modify the imputation'.

36 (2.1.115–16) *This . . . love:* 'This must be reported. If it were kept secret, the consequences of concealment would be grief exceeding the wrath that would be incurred if I divulged such love-matters.'

37 (2.2. S.D) *Enter POLONIUS.:* He enters without Ophelia, even though at 2.1.114 he had said to her 'Come, go we to the King.' That Shakespeare changed his mind is less surprising than that (according to the early texts) nobody removed the inconsistency, which is one of many in the play.

38 (2.2.98) *A foolish figure:* The rhetorical figure that he has employed here is predominantly 'gradatio', sustained anadiplosis (the last word of one clause becoming the first of the next). Here it incorporates 'antimetabole' (words repeated in inverse order), 'epizeuxis' (a word immediately duplicated) and 'ploce' (a word repeated within a line or a sequence of clauses).

39 (2.2.115–18) *'Doubt . . . love:* The sense of the poem is: 'Disbelieve that the stars are fire, disbelieve that the sun moves round the earth, suspect that truth is falsehood, but never disbelieve that I love.' In line 117, however, the shift in meaning of 'doubt' casts a shade of ambiguity over the assertion in line 118.

40 (2.2.136) *working . . . dumb:* 'silenced activity'. Q2 has 'working' but F1 has 'winking'.

41 (2.2.173) *a fishmonger:* (a) seller of fish; (b) pimp (because fish was sometimes associated with female flesh). Furthermore, fishmongers' wives and daughters were regarded as wanton and fertile.

42 (2.2.180–4) *For if the sun . . . look to't:* The gist is: 'The sun is
supposed to engender maggots in flesh (e.g. that of a dead dog,
which is good carrion for the sun's kiss); therefore your daughter
should not walk in the sun, lest she become pregnant.' (Perhaps
he hints that she should keep away from the royal son.)

43 (2.2.258–9) *Then . . . shadows:* Kittredge (pp. 187–8) offers this
gloss: 'If ambition is a shadow, our monarchs and heroes, who
are entirely composed of ambition, must be shadows, and our
beggars, the only persons in the world who have no ambition,
must alone be composed of real substance. If, now, the beggars
are the only real bodies, and the monarchs and heroes are
shadows, then the monarchs and heroes must be the shadows of
the beggars, since there cannot be a shadow without a real body
to cast it.'

44 (2.2.234–64) *Let me . . . attended:* This sequence is present in F1
but absent from Q1 and Q2.

45 (2.2.317–18) *the Lady . . . for't:* 'the Lady [played by a boy]
shall be allowed to speak without interruption – otherwise the
blank verse will limp unevenly'.

46 (2.2.323–4) *their inhibition . . . innovation:* (a) 'the prohibition
of their performing in the city is a consequence of the recent
disorder there'; (b) 'what hinders them from performing in the
city is the new fashion [for juvenile players]'.

47 (2.2.330) *eyrie of children:* The 'Children of the Chapel', a
company of boy actors at London's Blackfriars Theatre, became
fashionable in 1600 and 1601. (The Danish story is here infiltrated
by English cultural allusions.)

48 (2.2.328–51) *How comes . . . load too:* This material is present in
F1 but absent from Q2 and very briefly represented in Q1.

49 (2.2.368–69) *I am but . . . handsaw:* 'I am but mad north-north-
west' may mean: 'My mind is only slightly out of true, like a
compass-needle which points slightly to the west of north'.
Timothy Bright's *A Treatise of Melancholy*, 1586, explains that a
wind from the south and south-east is good for melancholy
people. 'I know a hawk from a handsaw' may mean: (i) 'I can at
least perceive obvious differences'; or (ii) 'I can make subtle
discriminations (a "hawk" being, like the handsaw, a workman's
tool, and a "handsaw" or hernshaw being, like the hawk, a bird)'.

50 (2.2.389) *scene individable, or poem unlimited:*   Editorial interpretations include: (a) 'plays with no breaks, or verse-dramas not
restricted by neoclassical conventions'; (b) 'both written and
improvised drama'; and (c) 'unclassifiable and all-inclusive plays'.

51 (2.2.389–90) *Seneca . . . Plautus . . . light:* Seneca was regarded
as the greatest Roman tragedian, and Plautus as the greatest
Roman writer of comedies.

52 (2.2.390–91) *For the law of writ and the liberty:* possibly: 'for
plays which observe the rules and plays which disregard them'.

53 (2.2.392) *Jephthah:* Judges 11 says that Jephthah promised God
that if he, Jephthah, defeated the Ammonites, he would sacrifice
the first thing to meet him on returning home. The 'first thing'
was Jephthah's only child, his daughter, whom he duly sacrificed.
Some Elizabethan ballads used this subject: one such ballad was
'Jepha [i.e. Jephthah,] Judge of Israel', which Hamlet proceeds
to quote. In it, the daughter laments that she must die a virgin.
See Jenkins, pp. 475–7.

54 (2.2.432–3) *as wholesome . . . than fine:* These words, represented only by 'as wholesome as sweete' in Q1, are present in
Q2 but absent from F1,

55 (2.2.434–5) *Aeneas' tale . . . slaughter:* The ultimate source of
this play-material is Aeneas's account to Dido (in Virgil's *Aeneid*,
Bk. II) of the sack of Troy, in which Priam, King of Troy, was
slaughtered by Pyrrhus, the Greek warrior.

56 (2.2.441) *ominous horse:* the wooden horse in which concealed
Greeks entered Troy.

57 (2.2.461) *senseless Ilium:* 'the inanimate citadel of Troy'.

58 (2.2.480) *strumpet Fortune:* The goddess Fortune is a 'strumpet'
because she is repeatedly unfaithful. As she turns her wheel,
human beings may fall from happiness to misery.

59 (2.2.538) *from her working:* 'as a result of the soul's operation'.
The soul (as in the Latin term, *anima*) was sometimes regarded as
female, though Richard II calls it male.

60 (2.2.568) *a dear father murdered:* Q1 has 'my deare father'; Q2
has 'a deere murthered'; and F1 has 'the Deere murthered'.

61 (2.2.584) *the devil:* Q1 has 'the Diuell', Q2 has 'a deale', and F1
has 'the Diuell'.

62 (2.2.587) *such spirits:* probably 'the vapours which engender weakness and melancholy'. (To interpret 'spirits' here as 'devils' would not accord with line 585.)

63 (3.1.1) *circumstance:* QI has 'meanes'; Q2 has 'conference' (which some editors prefer); FI has 'circumstance'. 'Drift of circumstance' could mean 'tendency of the course of conversation'.

64 (3.1.86) *pitch and moment:* 'lofty aim and importance'. FI has 'pith' (substance) where Q2 has 'pitch'. 'Pitch' could mean 'the height to which a falcon soared before swooping on its prey'.

65 (3.1.117–19) *virtue . . . you not:* 'even if virtue is grafted (like a slip or bud) on to our old sinful stock, we still retain the tang of sin. My love for you was thus negated by my corrupt nature.'

66 (3.1.168) *I have . . . determination:* The line is regular if the last word be pronounced hexasyllabically: 'de-tér-min-á-ti-òn'.

67 (3.1.170) *tribute:* In England, between the ninth and eleventh centuries, taxes were repeatedly imposed to pay the Danes. (This 'tribute' was a form of 'protection money'.)

68 (3.2.44) *it:* At this point, QI adds several lines in which Hamlet gives examples of clowns' catch-phrases (such as 'my coate wants a cullison' and 'your beere is sowre').

69 (3.2.112) *country matters:* (a) sexual intercourse (punning on the obscene term 'cunt'); (b) rural matters.

70 (3.2.116) *Nothing:* The figure nought and the term 'no-thing' could, in Shakespeare's day, refer to the vulva. ('Thing' could mean 'penis'.)

71 (3.2.124–5) *So long? . . . sables:* perhaps (a): 'So long ago? In that case, the Devil is welcome to my black cloak, for I should wear the fur coats that warm old men.'; or (b): 'As long as that? Then I don't need to borrow the Devil's black clothing, because I shall celebrate the fact that my father is still remembered by wearing the most splendid mourning-suit of fur that I can afford.'

72 (3.2.129–30) *hobby-horse . . . forgot:* The hobby-horse, used in morris dances and May games, was a dummy horse worn round the waist of a man. (Sometimes the term referred to the performer or his performance.) 'For O, for O, the hobby-horse is forgot' was the refrain of a ballad and was evidently a popular catch-phrase.

73 (3.2.132) *miching malicho:* 'mischief brewing'. QI has 'myching

Mallico', Q2 'munching *Mallico*', and F1 'Miching *Malicho*'. 'Miching' means 'lurking' (or 'loitering with intent'). 'Malicho' may derive from the Spanish *malheco* ('wrong-doing').

74 (3.2.137–9) *Be not . . . means:* 'If you are shameless enough to expose yourself, he will be shameless enough to tell you what the sexual consequences could be.'

75 (3.2.160–61) *women's fear . . . extremity:* 'women's fear and love are equivalent: nothing of either, or both in excess'. Line 159 is redundant (for its sense is absorbed by 160–61); and the fact that it does not rhyme indicates that it was a Shakespearian 'first thought' which was quickly superseded.

76 (3.2.164–5) *Where love . . . there:* This couplet is present in Q2 but absent from Q1 and F1.

77 (3.2.185–6) *Most necessary . . . debt:* 'It is most natural and inevitable that we forget to pay to ourselves debts of remembrance.'

78 (3.2.211–12) *To desperation . . . scope:* This couplet is present in Q2 but absent from Q1 and F1.

79 (3.2.230) *Marry, how? Tropically:* 'By St. Mary, how does that fit? Metaphorically.' Jenkins (p. 302) says that 'Marry trap' was apparently 'an exclamation of derision when a man was successfully tricked'. (Q1 has 'mary how trapically'; Q2 has 'mary how tropically'; and F1 has 'Marry, how? Tropically'.)

80 (3.2.230–32) *This play . . . Baptista:* Francesco Maria della Rovere, the Duke of Urbino (not of Vienna), was murdered in 1538, supposedly by poison in the ear. Luigi Gonzaga (not Gonzago) was the name of the instigator of the murder, and he was related to the Duchess, Leonora, formerly a Gonzaga. Hamlet's reference to a duke (after a *king* has appeared in *The Mousetrap*) suggests that Shakespeare has not fully adapted the historical story to the events in the play.

81 (3.2.235) *Let . . . unwrung:* 'A worn-out, saddle-sore horse may kick; our backs are sound.'

82 (3.2.238–9) *I could . . . dallying:* 'I could act as a puppet-master (providing the voices) to you and your lover, if I could see what you were both doing.'

83 (3.2.241–2) *take . . . worse:* 'Take off my edge' means both 'blunt the cutting-edge of my wit' and 'gratify my sexual ardour'. 'Still better and worse' means 'Even wittier but dirtier'.

84 (3.2.243) *So you mis-take your husbands:* 'In the marriage ceremony, women take their husbands "for better, for worse"; but they mis-take them, if worse follows (e.g., if the wife treacherously substitutes a different man for the husband).' Q1 has 'So you must take your husband;', Q2 has 'So you mistake your husbands.', and F1 has 'So you mistake Husbands.'.

85 (3.2.244–5) *'the croaking . . . revenge':* Hamlet telescopes two lines from the anonymous play *The True Tragedy of Richard III:* 'The screeking Rauen sits croking for reuenge. / Whole he[r]ds of beasts comes bellowing for reuenge.'

86 (3.2.266–9) *Would not . . . sir?:* 'If Fortune's treatment of me henceforth were as treacherous as a Christian who becomes a Turkish Muslim, wouldn't my success with the play, coupled with an abundantly-feathered hat and Provençal roses on my slashed shoes, enable me to become a member of a company of players?' (The 'Provençal roses' are large rosettes to conceal the ties of shoes. Q2 has 'prouinciall Roses'; F1 has 'Prouinciall Roses'. Some editors prefer to interpret the phrase as 'roses of Provins': see Jenkins, p. 509.)

87 (3.2.272–6) *For . . . rhymed:* The gist of the song is that Jove's realm has been stripped and usurped by a clown (a reference to the usurping Claudius). 'Pajock' may mean 'patchcock' (clown, oaf) or 'peacock' (vain showy creature). The missing rhyme is 'ass'.

88 (3.2.330–31) *'While . . . musty:* The 'somewhat musty' proverb is: 'While the grass grows, the horse starves' (implying: 'I, the Prince, would like the throne now').

89 (3.3.15) *The cess of majesty:* 'The decease of a king's reign', i.e. the death of a king. Some editors prefer 'cease' to 'cess'. (Q2 has 'the cesse of Maiestie'; F1 has 'the cease of Maiestie'.)

90 (3.3.37) *primal eldest curse:* God said that Cain was 'cursed from the earth' for slaying his brother Abel (Genesis 4:11).

91 (3.3.79) *hire . . . revenge:* Q1 has 'a benefit, And not reuenge'; Q2 has 'base and silly, not reuendge'; and F1 has 'hyre and Sallery, not Reuenge'.

92 (3.4.48–50) *Yea . . . act:* 'Yes, even this solid earth itself (compounded of four elements), with a face as sad as if it beheld Doomsday, is sick with thinking about the deed.'

93 (3.4.70–75) *Sense sure . . . difference:* This passage is present in Q2 but absent from Q1 and F1. Lines 73–5, from 'Nor sense' to 'a difference', mean: 'and common sense was never so subjugated by derangement as to fail to retain some modicum of selectivity to employ when the contrast was so evident'.

94 (3.4.77–80) *Eyes without . . . mope:* This passage is present in Q2 but absent from Q1 and F1.

95 (3.4.86) *frost . . . burn:* 'apparently chilled ardour can become actively ardent'

96 (3.4.119–20) *Your . . . end:* 'the normally-prone hairs on your head start up and stand erect, like outgrowths come to life.'

97 (3.4.136–7) *This bodiless . . . in:* 'Madness is very cunning in its creation of such figments of the imagination.' Near this point, in Q1 the Queen proceeds: 'But as I haue a soule, I sweare by heauen, / I neuer knew of this most horride murder.'

98 (3.4.146–8) *It will . . . unseen:* 'That will merely let a thin layer of skin or membrane cover the ulcerous place, while foul corruption, undermining everything, invisibly spreads the infection.'

99 (3.4.160–64) *That monster . . . put on:* These lines are present in Q2 but absent from Q1 and F1. Q1 subsequently offers an exchange of dialogue in which Hamlet says, '[M]other, but assist me in reuenge, / And in his death your infamy shall die', and the Queen replies that she will consent to, and conceal, '[w]hat stratagem soe're thou shalt deuise'.

100 (3.4.168) *house:* Q1 and F1 lack the passage from 'the next more easy' to 'potency'. Q2 gives it but lacks a verb here, so I have supplied one, 'house' (which fits the sense and the alliterative patterns). Other conjectures by editors include 'shame', 'curb' and 'lodge'. (See Jenkins, pp. 522–3.)

101 (3.4.192–5) *Unpeg . . . down:* The 'famous ape' is now unknown; but Hamlet is evidently alluding to a story in which an ape, on seeing birds fly away when released from a basket on a house-top, tried to emulate them – with fatal results. Hamlet thus warns Gertrude not to attempt to release his secret to Claudius. ('To try conclusions' means 'to experiment'.)

102 (3.4.201–9) *There's letters . . . meet:* These lines are present in
Q2 but absent from Q1 and F1.

103 (4.1. S.D.) *ACT 4, SCENE 1:* In 1676, a late Quarto introduced
this division, and editors have customarily maintained it. The
action, however, should be continuous, the Queen remaining
in her chamber. (Q2 directs the Queen to enter at the
beginning of what is now Act 4, scene 1, but this seems
unnecessary and erroneous.)

104 (4.1.40) *So haply slander:* This is a conventional editorial
conjecture to fill a gap in the sense. (Jenkins, p. 336, proposes
'So envious slander'.)

105 (4.1.41–4) *Whose . . . air:* These lines are present in Q2 but
absent from Q1 and F1.

106 (4.2.16–18) *he keeps . . . swallowed:* 'just as an ape keeps food
in a corner of his jaw, letting a long time elapse between taking
it in and swallowing it, so the King patronises these officials for
a long time before getting rid of them'.

107 (4.3.4–5) *the distracted . . . eyes:* 'the feckless masses, who
injudiciously love a person who merely is outwardly attrac-
tive'.

108 (4.3.9) *Deliberate pause:* 'the result of careful deliberation'.

109 (4.3.25–7) *Alas . . . worm:* These lines are present in Q2,
have a briefer counterpart in Q1, and are absent from F1.

110 (4.3.49) *cherub:* Cherubim were supposed to have keen vision. (Hamlet hints that he is aware of Claudius's lethal
intentions.)

111 (4.3.52–3) *man . . . flesh:* according to Genesis 2:24, Matthew
19:5–6, and Mark 10:8.

112 (4.4. S.D.) *Open . . . army:* In Q1, the stage direction is:
'*Enter Fortenbrasse, Drumme and Souldiers.*' In Q2, it is: '*Enter
Fortinbrasse with his Army ouer the stage.*' In F1, it is: '*Enter
Fortinbras with an Armie.*'

113 (4.4.54) *Is not to stir . . . argument:* The intended sense
requires an additional 'not' ('Is *not* not to stir'). Hamlet intends
to say that the truly great person is able to act without needing
a great cause.

114 (4.4.9–66) *Good sir . . . worth!:* These lines appear in Q2 but
not in Q1 or F1.

115 (4.5.19–20) *So full . . . spilt:* 'Guilty people are so full of naïve mistrust that, in their very fear of being found out, they reveal their guilt and betray themselves.'

116 (4.5.25–6) *By his . . . shoon:* The insignia of a pilgrim included a straw hat with a scallop-shell (rather than a 'cockle') fixed to it, a staff, and sandals. Lovers were conventionally depicted as pilgrims seeking a (secular) female saint. (Romeo is evidently disguised as a pilgrim when he meets Juliet: see *Romeo and Juliet*, Act 1, scene 5.)

117 (4.5.40–41) *the owl . . . daughter:* The allusion is apparently to a folk-tale in which Jesus turned a baker's daughter into an owl as punishment for her niggardliness.

118 (4.5.49) *Valentine:* i.e. 'sweetheart': for an ancient tradition held (with variants) that the first person of the opposite sex whom one saw on St Valentine's Day (February 14th) became thereby one's sweetheart.

119 (4.5.87) *Feeds . . . clouds:* 'increases his bewilderment, keeps himself preoccupied by vague uncertainties'. F1 has 'his wonder', whereas Q2 has 'this wonder'.

120 (4.5.90–92) *Wherein . . . ear:* 'in which connection the scandal-mongers, lacking hard facts, necessarily do not flinch from filling ear after ear with accusations against myself'.

121 (4.5.133–6) *To this . . . father:* 'This is my standpoint: I care nothing for this world or the next, come what may; but I'm determined to avenge my father thoroughly.'

122 (4.5.142–3) *swoopstake . . . loser?:* O.E.D. explains that 'swoopstake', corresponding to the current 'sweepstake', was a term for the act of taking all the stakes in the game, or for the person who does so. Laertes, who seizes the innocent along with the guilty, resembles someone who takes all the stakes and not merely allotted winnings. (Q1 has 'Swoop-stake-like', Q2 has 'soopstake', and F1 has 'Soop-stake'.)

123 (4.5.146–7) *like . . . blood:* According to legend, the pelican fed its young with blood from its own breast, having first stabbed the breast with its beak.

124 (4.5.161–63) *Nature . . . loves:* 'Love makes an individual's nature keenly sensitive; and, when it is sensitive, it sends some precious part of itself after the (absent) object of its love' (the

'object' being Polonius, in Laertes' view). These lines are present in F1 but absent from Q1 and Q2.

125 (4.5.170–71) *You must . . . it!:* 'Adown adown' and 'Call him adown-a' are refrains in ballads of that time. 'Wheel' meant 'refrain'.

126 (4.5.173) *This . . . matter:* 'This nonsense is more telling than sense.'

127 (4.5.174–6) *There's rosemary . . . thoughts:* The rosemary and pansies are presented to Laertes; rosemary being indeed a symbol of remembrance, while the name 'pansies' derives from the French *pensées*, meaning 'thoughts'.

128 (4.5.179–80) *[to the King:] There's fennel . . . rue for you:* Q1, Q2 and F1 provide no directions specifying who gets what here. Some editors think that the fennel and columbines signify marital infidelity and are therefore given to the Queen, whereas rue (for regret or pentience) is given to the King; but others think that fennel (flattery) and columbines (cuckoldry) are more appropriate for the King, and rue is more appropriate for the Queen. Of the subsequent flowers, Jenkins (p. 359) remarks: 'The *daisy* is the flower of (unhappy) love, *violets* of faithfulness.'

129 (S.D.) *SCENE 6:* In Q1, the scene that ensues is a dialogue in which Horatio tells the Queen that Hamlet has eluded the King's murderous scheme and has returned. She says that (in order to help Hamlet) she will allay the suspicions of the treacherous King, and adds:

> [C]ommend me
> A mother's care to him, bid him a while
> Be wary of his presence, lest that he
> Faile in that he goes about.

130 (4.7.20) *spring . . . stone:* Wood may appear to be petrified (turned to stone) if a spring deposits minerals (e.g. limestone) on it.

131 (4.7.56) *'Thus diest thou.':* Q1 has 'thus he dies.', Q2 has 'Thus didst thou.', and F1 has 'Thus diddest thou.'

132 (4.7.67–80) *My lord . . . graveness:* This material is present in Q2 but absent from Q1 and F1.

133 (4.7.86–7) *As . . . beast:* 'as if (like a centaur) he shared his body and nature with the splendid animal'.

134 (4.7.88) *in . . . tricks:* 'however much I strove to imagine his postures and feats of skill'.

135 (4.7.91) *Lamord:* The name resembles *La Mort*: Death.

136 (4.7.99–101) *the scrimers . . . them:* These lines are present in Q2 but absent from Q1 and F1. ('Scrimers' means 'fencers'.)

137 (4.7.115–17) *And nothing . . . much:* 'and nothing is constantly good, for goodness may perish from excess, as if it had caught pleurisy'. (Pleurisy was thought to result from excess of blood or fluid.)

138 (4.7.113–22) *There lives . . . ulcer:* These lines are present in Q2 but absent from Q1 and F1.

139 (4.7.139–47) *And, for . . . death:* In Q1, it is the King who proposes the application of poison to the rapier.

140 (4.7.169) *a grosser name:* e.g. 'priests'-pintles': priests' penises.

141 (4.7.171) *crownet weeds:* garlanded wild flowers.

142 (4.7.187–8) *When . . . out:* 'When I have shed these tears, the feminine aspect of my nature will be gone.'

143 (5.1.2) *salvation:* He means 'damnation'. Suicide was regarded as a mortal sin, and a person deemed guilty of suicide would normally not be granted Christian burial in consecrated ground with customary rites.

144 (5.1.4–5) *The crowner . . . burial:* 'The coroner has conducted an inquest and concluded that she is eligible for Christian burial.'

145 (5.1.9) *se offendendo:* his version of *se defendendo*, a legal term for 'killing in self-defence'.

146 (5.1.13) *goodman delver:* 'Mister Digger'.

147 (5.1.21) *crowner's quest law:* the law governing coroners' inquests.

148 (5.1.32) *bore arms:* (a) 'had a coat of arms, the sign of a gentleman'; (b) 'had arms on his shoulders'. The following few lines, from 'Why' to 'without arms?', are present in F1 but absent from Q1 and Q2.

149 (5.1.37–8) *confess . . . to:* The grave-digger's companion interrupts the proverb with 'Go to' (i.e., 'Go on with the

question', 'Come to the point') because the proverb, in full, is: 'Confess thyself and be hanged.'

150 (5.1.58) *Yaughan:* presumably the name of the proprietor of a tavern near the theatre. He is named in F1 but not in Q1 or Q2.

151 (5.1.61) *O . . . a:* The 'O' and 'a' may represent sounds uttered in time to his digging.

152 (5.1.59–62) *In youth . . . meet:* These are garbled parts of 'The Aged Lover Renounceth Love', a lyric by Thomas, Lord Vaux.

153 (5.1.70) *intil the land:* 'into the earth'.

154 (5.1.75–6) *o'er-reaches:* Q2 has 'ore-reaches'; F1 has 'o're Offices'. Some editors choose the latter, rendered as 'o'er-offices', meaning 'lords it over (by virtue of his office)'.

155 (5.1.86–8) *Did . . . with them?:* 'Was the development of these bones so easy and inexpensive that they are of value only for skittles?'

156 (5.1.97–8) *tell . . . battery:* 'threaten him with prosecution for assault'.

157 (5.1.184–5) *let . . . come:* 'even if she applies her cosmetics one inch deep, this is how her face will look eventually'.

158 (5.1.194) *Alexander:* Alexander the Great (356–323 BC), King of Macedonia.

159 (5.1.203) *Caesar:* Julius Caesar (*c.*102–44 BC), Roman ruler.

160 (5.1.220) *last trumpet:* the trumpet-blast that wakes the dead at Doomsday.

161 (5.1.230) *May violets spring:* Violets are emblematic of both faithful love and chastity.

162 (5.1.243–4) *T'o'ertop . . . Olympus:* According to Greek mythology, giants attempted to scale Olympus, the mountain of the gods, by piling Mount Ossa upon Mount Pelion.

163 (5.1.245–7) *whose . . . hearers:* 'whose lamentation, like a magician's conjuration, causes the planets to stop in their course like hearers stricken with amazement'.

164 (5.1.248) *Hamlet the Dane:* (a) 'Hamlet, true King of Denmark'; (b) 'Hamlet of the royal Danish line'.

165 (5.1.271–3) *till . . . wart:* 'until our mass of earth is so high that it singes its head against the sun's sphere and makes Mount Ossa seem tiny as a wart'.

166 (5.1.281–2) *Let . . . day:* 'Hercules may rant as much as he likes, but lesser creatures remain unaffected.' (Hamlet implies: 'My day will come.')

167 (5.1.287) *living monument:* (a) enduring monument; (b) life-like statue; (c) sacrificial memorial (in the sense that Hamlet, now living, will be killed in revenge).

168 (5.2.36) *It . . . service:* 'it served me as effectively as a yeoman [a brave countryman]'.

169 (5.2.41) *As peace . . . wear:* 'as Peace should continue to wear her garland of wheat' (this garland being a traditional emblem of the bounty of peace-time).

170 (5.2.42) *stand a commere:* Q2 and F1 have 'stand a Comma'; Q1 has no equivalent. Editorial interpretations of 'stand a Comma' include: 'make a pause', 'hold their interests separate but still connected', 'be small and insignificant' and 'be a link' The emendation, 'stand a commere', seems preferable, for 'commere', meaning 'godmother or patroness', maintains the feminine imagery of the previous line.

171 (5.2.43) *ases of great charge:* (a) 'other highly significant clauses introduced by "as"'; (b) 'asses bearing heavy burdens'.

172 (5.2.57) *Why . . . employment:* This line is present in F1 but absent from Q1 and Q2.

173 (5.2.68–70) *And . . . evil:* 'And isn't it damnable, to let the person who is a cancer within human nature proceed further in his evil course?'

174 (5.2.74) *And . . . 'one':* 'and a man's life is so short that it's over before you can say the word "one" '.

175 (5.2.68–80) *To quit . . . here?:* These lines appear in F1 but are absent from Q2. Q1 has four lines in which Hamlet regrets his conduct to Laertes.

176 (5.2.85–6) *Let . . . mess:* 'If a beastly person owns much livestock, his manger will stand alongside a king's table' (i.e., his wealth will enable him to dine alongside the monarch). This suggests that 'chough' in line 87 is an alternative spelling of 'chuff', meaning 'a boorish but wealthy rural person'. Nevertheless, the other meaning of 'chough' – 'a bird of the crow family, especially a jackdaw, and hence a chatterer' – fits Osric's manner of speech.

177 (5.2.110) *dizzy*:   Q2 (copies of which differ) gives both 'dosie'
and 'dazzie'. Q3 gives 'dizzie'. Q1 and F1 have no counterparts.
Jenkins (p. 401) reads 'dozy' ('bewilder, stupefy').

178 (5.2.102–30) *Sir, here . . . sir?*:   These lines are present in Q2
but absent from Q1 and F1.

179 (5.2.132–6) *I dare . . . unfellowed*:   These lines are present in
Q2 but absent from Q1 and F1.

180 (5.2.156–8) *in a dozen . . . nine*:   'in a dozen bouts, he will not
score three more hits than you. He has bet that Laertes will
score no more than twelve against your nine.' (The arithmetic
of Osric or Claudius or Shakespeare may be confused.)

181 (5.2.174) *The lapwing . . . head*:   'Like a lapwing-chick
running about with its eggshell on its head, this courtier runs
off wearing his hat (at last).'

182 (5.2.175) *He did . . . sucked it*:   'He even bowed politely to his
mother's nipple before he sucked it.'

183 (5.2.177–9) *only got . . . collection*:   'acquired merely the
fashionable turns of speech and, from a custom of polite
address, a collection of frothy utterances'.

184 (5.2.180) *fanned and winnowed opinions*:   Q2 has 'prophane
and trennowed opinions'; F1 has 'fond and winnowed
opinions'; Q1 has no equivalent. 'Fanned and winnowed'
means 'refined and sifted': the image is that of separating wheat
from chaff during the winnowing process.

185 (5.2: from start of S.D. after 181 to end of S.D. at 193) Enter a
LORD . . . Exit Lord.:   These lines are present in Q2 but
absent from F1. Q1 has three lines in which a gentleman tells
Hamlet that the King, Queen and courtiers are assembling.

186 (5.2.204–5) *There is . . . sparrow*:   Matthew 10:29 (Geneva
Bible): 'Are not two sparrowes sold for a farthing, and one of
them shal not fall on the ground without your Father?'

187 (5.2.207–9) *Since . . . be*:   'As no dead man knows what he is
leaving behind, does it mater if one departs early? Accept it.'

188 (5.2.228–9) *That I . . . brother*:   'that you may consider that I,
like an archer who shot too far and wounded his brother,
harmed you accidentally'. Q1 and Q2 have 'my brother'; F1
has 'my Mother'.

189 (5.2.233–5) *Till . . . ungored:* 'until senior experts in the tradition of honourable conduct tell me that, for such reconciliation, there are precedents which will prevent me from disgracing myself '.

190 (5.2.334) *I am . . . Dane:* 'I am more like an ancient Roman than a Dane (for I am prepared to prove my loyalty by committing suicide).'

191 (5.2.382–3) *I have . . . invite me:* 'I have some unforgotten rights to this kingdom, and my favourable situation invites me to claim them now.'

192 (5.2.385) *from . . . more:* 'shall report the words of him, Hamlet, whose vote for you will attract other supporters'.

193 (5.2.387–8) *lest . . . happen:* 'lest there occur more mishaps, in addition to (or as a result of) plotting and blunders'.

194 (5.2.395) *Becomes . . . amiss:* 'is appropriate to a battlefield but appears very inappropriate here'.

GLOSSARY

Where a pun or an ambiguity is apparent, the meanings are distinguished as (a) and (b), or (a), (b) and (c), etc. Otherwise, alternative meanings are distinguished as (i) and (ii), or as (i), (ii) and (iii), etc. Abbreviations include the following: adj., adjective; adv., adverb; cf., compare; e.g., for example; esp., especially; *O.E.D.*, *Oxford English Dictionary*; vb., verb.

a (as pronoun): he.

About, my brains: 'My intelligence, get busy'.

abridgement: 2.2.408: (a) dramatic pastime; (b) curtailment.

absolute: (i: 5.1.129:) certain; (ii: 5.2.104:) perfect.

abstract: epitome.

abuse (noun): 4.7.49: deception, imposture.

abuse (vb.): impose upon, deceive.

act: 1.2.205: effect, operation.

action of battery: lawsuit concerning an unlawful attack by beating or wounding.

addition: (i: 1.4.20, 2.1.46:) title, style of address; (ii: 4.4.17:) embellishment (literally, heraldic addition).

admiration: wonder.

advantage: superiority.

aery: nestful of young hawks.

affection: 3.1.162: (a) inclination; (b) emotion.

affront: confront.

aim: 4.5.9: guess.

amaze: 2.2.549: bewilder.

amazement: (i: 3.2.314:) astonishment; (ii: 3.4.110:) bewilderment.

ambition: (a) inordinate desire for distinction; (b) ostentatious glory.

anchor's cheer: anchorite's lifestyle.

angle (noun): fishing-hook.

answer (noun): (i: 5.2.160: a) reply; (b) acceptance of a challenge; (ii: 5.2.254:) riposte: return hit in fencing.

answer (vb.): 3.4.175: (a) justify; (b) atone for; **be answered**: be defended.

antic: odd, strange.

apoplexed: paralysed.

appliance: remedial application.

appointment: equipment.

apprehension: (i: 2.2.300:) comprehension; (ii: 4.1.11:) conception.

approve: (i: 1.1.29:) corroborate; (ii: 5.2.130:) commend.

appurtenance: 2.2.360: accompaniment.

argal (version of Latin *ergo*): therefore.

argument: (i: 2.2.345, 3.2.225:) plot of a play; (ii: 4.4.54:) cause of contention.

arithmetic of memory: mental arithmetic.

arm (vb.): prepare.

arrest: 2.2.67: staying order.

artere: sinew, ligament.

article: of great article: of great importance.

artless: unskilful, naïve.

ases: 5.2.43: (a) plural of 'as'; (b) asses.

askant: sideways.

assay (noun): (i: 2.2.71:) assault; (ii: 3.3.69:) trial, attempt. Assay of bias: indirect attempt.

assay (vb.): 3.1.14: test the inclination of.

assigns (noun): appendages.

assume: take on, adopt.

assurance: 5.1.111: (a) security; (b) legal deed securing possession of land.

at foot: closely.

attribute (noun): reputation.

audit: official inspection of accounts.

auspicious: cheerful.

back: 4.7.152: backer-up, second string.

baked meats: pies and other pastry.

bands: bonds, obligations.

Barbary horse: small but swift horse.

barked about: encrusted.

bare: 3.1.76: (a) unsheathed; (b) mere.

barren: 3.2.40: dull-witted.

bated: (i: 4.7.137, 5.2.311:) blunted; (ii: 5.2.23:) excepted.

batten: feed abundantly.

beat: 3.1.174: think intently, concentrate.

beautified: endowed with beauty.

beaver: visor.

bedded: flat.

beetle (vb.): overhang.

beget: produce.

bend (vb.): incline.

bent (noun): limit of capacity.

berattle: fill with din.

bestir: get to work

beteem: permit.

betimes: in good time.

better (vb.): improve; perfect oneself.

bevy: 5.2.176: flock of birds; hence, company.

bias: in bowls, the lead weight which makes the bowl take a devious course.

bilboes: iron shackles attached to a horizontal bar; used to confine prisoners in a ship.

bisson: blinding.

blank (noun): 4.1.42: (a) target at point-blank range; (b) white disk in the centre of a target; hence goal.

blank (vb.): blanch.

blast in proof: burst when tested.

blastment: shrivelling.

blaze (noun): momentary outburst.

blazon (vb.): proclaim.

blench: flinch.

blood: *in blood*: in the vigour of youth.

blown: blooming; **broad blown**: in full bloom.

board (vb.): accost.

bodkin: small dagger.

bond: pledge.

bore (noun): calibre of a gun; hence: size, importance.

borne in hand: deceived.

botch up: put together clumsily.

brainish: headstrong.

bravery: bravado, ostentatious display.

breathe: 1.3.130: speak.

breathing time: time for taking exercise.

breed (noun): species.

bringing home: burial.

broad: gross, unrestrained.

broker: 1.3.127: (a) middleman; (b) pimp.

brooch: conspicuous ornament (because worn in the hat).

bruit (vb.): 1.2.127: noisily proclaim.

bug: bogy: imaginary horror.

bulk: bodily frame.

burial: 5.1.24: a grave.

burning zone: orbit in which the sun moves.

button: (i: 1.3.40:) bud; (ii: 2.2.225:) knob at the top of a cap.

buzz!: interjection meaning 'That's already known!'.

buzzers: scandal-mongers.

by'r Lady: 'by our Lady [Saint Mary]'.

calendar: register, account book.

calf: extreme fool.

candied: sugared.

canker (noun): (i: 1.3.39:) canker-worm: a caterpillar or other insect larva which destroys buds and leaves; (ii: 5.2.69: a) cancer; (b) spreading sore or ulcer.

canon: religious edict.

canonized: consecrated.

can well: can do well, are skilled.

capable of: susceptible to.

cap-à-pie (from French *de cap à pied*): from head to foot.

capon: castrated and fattened cock; hence, dull fellow.

carbuncle: fiery-coloured gem.

card: *by the card*: according to the points on a mariner's compass; hence, exactly to the point.

carefully: 1.1.6: punctiliously, punctually.

carp (noun): species of fresh-water fish.

carriage: (i: 1.1.94:) execution, completion; (ii: 5.2.145:) affected word for 'hanger' (strap).

carries them through and through: 5.2.179: sustains them when encountering all.

carrion: dead flesh.

carry it away: be victorious.

cart: chariot.

carve for oneself: do as one wishes.

cast (noun): (i: 1.1.73:) casting, founding; (ii: 3.1.85) tinge, hue.

cast beyond ourselves: over-run the trail, go too far.

cataplasm: poultice.

cautel: deceit.

censure: opinion, judgement.

centre: 2.2.158: middle of the earth.

cerements: literally, waxed wrappings for the dead; hence, grave-clothes.

cess: decease, cessation.

chameleon: small lizard which supposedly fed on air.

changeling: 5.2.53: child which, supposedly, fairies left in place of the child they stole; hence, substitute.

chanson (from French): song, ballad.

character (vb.): imprint, inscribe.

charge (noun): (i: 4.4.47:) cost; (ii: 5.2.43: a) importance; (b) burden. **Gives the charge**: makes the attack.

choler: 3.2.292: (a) bile; (b) anger.

chopine: shoe raised on a very thick sole.

chopless: without the lower jaw (chop or chap).

chorus: actor who explains or summarises the dramatic action.

chough: 5.2.87: (a) bird of the crow family, esp. a jackdaw; hence, a chatterer; (b) boorish but wealthy fellow.

cicatrice: scar of a wound.

circumstance: (i: 1.5.127:) circumlocution, discussion; (ii: 2.2.156; 3.3.83:) evidence.

clepe: call, name.

climature: region.

close (adj.): secret.

closely: secretly.

close with: engage in conversation.

clouds: in clouds: in obscurity.

clouts: cloths, clothes.

Cock: by Cock: 4.5.59: (a, euphemism for) by God; (b, possibly) for fornication.

cockle-hat: pilgrim's hat bearing a cockle-shell (normally a scallop-shell).

coil (noun): 3.1.67: (a) fleshly enfolding; (b) bustle, turmoil.

colleagued: allied.

collection: (i: 4.5.9:) gathering by inference; (ii: 5.2.179:) assortment of phrases.

colour (noun): 3.4.128: (a) character; (b) colour.

colour (vb.): (i: 2.2.275:) disguise; (ii: 3.1.45:) justify.

columbine: climbing plant with flower considered an emblem of cuckoldry.

co-meddled: mixed together.

come tardy off: fall short.

commend: (i: 5.2.170:) offer; (ii: 5.2.172:) praise; **commended him to you**: greeted you.

comment: 3.2.78: critical attention.

commerce: 3.1.109: (a) social intercourse; (b) trade.

commere: godmother, patroness.

companies: 2.2.14: companion-ship.

compare with: vie with.

competent: 1.1.90: commensu-rate, equal.

complexion: (i: 1.4.27:) aspect of temperament; (ii: 5.2.96:) constitution.

comply: 'observe the formalities of courtesy' (O.E.D.).

conceit: (i: 2.2.537, 541; 3.4.112:) imagination; (ii: 5.2.145: a) ingenuity; (b) design.

conceit upon: fanciful preoccupation with.

conception: 2.2.183: (a) understanding; (b) pregnancy.

concernancy: import, relevance.

concerning (noun): 3.4.190: concern.

conclusion: try conclusions: experiment.

condolement: grief.

confederate: conspiring to assist.

conference: conversation.

confine (noun): place of confinement.

congrue: agree, accord.

conjunctive: closely connected (resembling twin planets).

conscience: 3.1.83: (a) inner voice of moral judgement; (b) reflectiveness.

considered: suitable for consideration.

consonancy: agreement. **Consonancy of our youth**: 2.2.279-80: (a) our being of the same youthful age; (b) our harmonious relationship when young.

continent: (i: 4.4.64:) container; (ii: 5.2.107: a) summary, embodiment; (b) geographical continent.

contraction: contractual relations.

conveyance: (i: 4.4.3:) expediting of movement; (ii: 5.1.105:) contract for the transference of ownership.

convoy: transport.

cope: encounter, meet.

core: corpse.

couch: lie low, hide.

counsel (noun): 4.2.10: (a) advice; (b) secret.

count (noun): 4.7.17: account, reckoning.

countenance: 4.2.14: favour, patronage.

counter: 4.5.110: following a scent in the wrong direction; hence, misguided.

counterfeit presentment: representation in an image or portrait.

country (adj.): 3.2.112: (a) sexual; (b) rural.

couplets: the two fledglings of the dove.

cousin: kinsman (of any kind except parent, child, brother or sister).

cov'nant: covenant, legal obligation.

cozen: cheat.

cozenage: 5.2.67: (a) cheating, deception; (b) cousinage, kinship.

cracked within the ring: 2.2.416: (a) no longer legal tender, like a coin cracked or clipped within the circle round the monarch's head; (b, of a boy's voice) broken, and thus useless for female rôles.

crants (cf. German *Kranz*): garland, chaplet.

crescent: growing.

cross (vb.): confront, intercept.

crow-flower: (probably) ragged robin.

crowner: coroner.

crownet: coronet.

cry (noun): pack (e.g. of hounds).

cry on havoc: 5.2.357: proclaim wholesale slaughter.

cunning (noun): skill, wisdom, dexterity.

curb: bow, bend.

currents: courses of events.

Damon: faithful friend (referring to the classical story of Damon and Phintias).

Dansker: Dane.

days of nature: days of one's life.

dear: (i: 3.4.190:) important, vital; (5.2.144:) rare, precious.

dearest: 1.2.182: direst, most cruel.

dearth: dearness, high cost.

debate (vb.): dispute, contend.

declension: decline, deterioration.

defeat: 5.2.58: destruction. **Make defeat upon**: ruin, destroy.

defeated: 1.2.10: (a) disfigured, defaced; (b) frustrated.

defence: fencing.

definement: specification.

devise: explain.

diction: description.

diet: nourishment.

difference: 4.5.182, 5.2.104: distinction.

digested: ordered, arranged.

dilated: set out at length.

directions: 2.1.63: courses to the goal or object.

disappointed: 1.5.77: without confession and absolution, and therefore unprepared for death.

disastering: blighting.

disclose (noun): disclosure of a young bird when its shell breaks; hence, disclosure of what is hatching.

disclose (vb.): hatch.

discourse, discourse of reason: logical reasoning.

discovery: disclosure.

dismal: calamitous.

dismantle: divert.

dispatch: (i: 1.5.75:) deprive; (ii. 3.3.3:) execute swiftly.

disprized: unvalued.

distemper: 'deranged or dis- ordered condition of the body or mind' (*O.E.D.*).

distempered: 3.2.290-92: (a) ill in body or mind; (b) intoxicated.

distracted: confusedly irrational.

distrust (vb.): fear for.

divide inventorially: classify in detail.

divulging: becoming publicly known.

dizzy (vb.): bewilder, make giddy.

document: 4.5.177: piece of instruction.

doubt: (i: 1.2.254, 2.2.117, 3.1.166:) suspect; (ii: 2.2.115, 116, 118:) disbelieve. **In doubt**: 4.5.6: ambiguous.

dout (vb.): extinguish.

down-gyvèd: fallen down to the ankles.

draw: 3.4.215: (a) proceed; (b) drag.

draw on more: bring others.

drift (noun): (i: 2.1.37; 4.7.150:) purpose, plot; (ii: 3.1.1:) tendency, direction.

drossy: worthless.

dup (vb.): open.

duty: respect.

eager: sharp, sour.

easiness: (i: 3.4.165:) facility; (ii: 5.1.65:) indifference.

ecstasy: madness.

edge: (i: 3.1.26:) stimulus; (ii: 3.2.241: a) cutting edge; (b) sexual desire.

effect: (i: 1.5.64:) operative influence; (ii: 3.3.54:) acquisition; (iii: 3.4.127:) intention.

eisel: vinegar.

enacture: fulfilment.

encompassment: talking around a subject.

encounter: manner of addressing or accosting.

encumbered: folded.

ends: results.

engaged: entangled.

engineer: military engineer, sapper.

enseamèd: greasy.

entreatment: conversation, interview.

envious: malicious, spiteful.

enviously: maliciously.

equivocation: exploitation of ambiguities.

erring: wandering.

escot: maintain.

espials: spies.

essentially: basically.

estate: authority, rank.

even: 2.2.282: straightforward.

even-Christian: fellow-Christian.

event: issue, consequence.

exception: disapproval, objection.

excrement: outgrowth (e.g. hair).

exercise: 3.1.45: religious practice.

exeunt: they go out.

exit: he or she goes out.

expostulate: debate, discourse upon.

express (adj.): direct, purposive.

extent: condescension.

extravagant: wandering beyond bounds, vagrant.

eyas: young hawk.

eye: in his eye: in his presence; I have an eye of you: I am watching you.

false fire: weapons firing only blanks.

familiar: friendly.

fancy: (i: 1.3.71:) excessive ornamentation; (ii: 5.2.144:) fanciful taste.

fantasy: imagination.

fardel: burden, bundle.

farm (vb.): rent.

fashion of himself: his usual behaviour.

fat: 5.2.279: (a) sweaty; (b) plump, overweight.

fatness: grossness.

favour: (i: 1.3.5:) fondness; (ii: 5.1.184: a) appearance (esp. facial); (b) beauty.

fear (noun): 3.3.8: solicitude, concern.

fear (vb.): 1.3.51, 3.4.7, 4.5.122: fear for.

feat: evil deed.

feature: physique.

fee: in fee: freehold, with absolute possession.

fell-incensed: fiercely angered.

felly: one of the curved pieces forming the rim of a wheel.

fetch (noun): device.

fierce: violent.

find: (i: 3.1.185:) discover the secret of; (ii: 5.1.8:) return as a verdict.

fine (noun): (i: 5.1.100:) legal action to transfer ownership of an estate; (ii: 5.1.101:) end.

fine (adj.): (i: 2.2.433, 4.5.161:) exquisite, subtle; (ii: 5.1.102:) handsome; (iii: 5.1.102:) powdery.

fine: in fine: finally.

finger (vb.): purloin.

fishmonger: 2.2.173: (a) vendor of fish; (b) pimp; (c) man whose womenfolk are wanton and fecund.

flaw: sudden squall of wind.

flush (adj.): lusty.

flushing: redness.

foil: (i: 2.2.314, 5.2.250:) rapier for fencing, usually with a blunted edge and tip, sometimes with a button at the tip; (ii: 5.2.240: a) fencing-rapier; (b) setting which by contrast enhances a jewel.

fond: foolish.

fools of nature: dupes or playthings of nature.

foot: at foot: closely.

forced cause: by reason of compulsion.

fordo: destroy.

forest of feathers: plumes worn by actors of tragedy.

forestalled: prevented.

forgery: invention.

form (noun): (i: 1.4.30, 2.2.299, 541:) appearance, expression; (ii: 1.5.100:) image.

frame (noun): (i: 3.2.296:) form, order; (ii: 5.1.41: a) framework of the gallows; (b) framework of a house.

frankly: freely, without constraint.

free: (i: 2.2.548, 3.2.234:) guiltless; (ii: 2.2.270, 4.3.62:) voluntary, unconstrained.

fret: 3.2.359: (a) equip with frets (markers for the fingering); (b) irritate.

fretted: embossed.

friending: friendship.

front (noun): brow.

frontier: frontier town or fortress.

fruit: dessert.

fruitful: copious.

function: bearing or action during performance.

fust: grow mouldy.

gaged: engaged, staked.

gain-giving misgiving.

gait: progress.

gall (vb.): (i: 1.3.39:) mar; (ii: 4.7.146:) graze; (iii: 5.1.133:) make sore by chafing.

galled: sore from rubbing or chafing.

gambol: jump.

garb: manner.

gather and surmise: consider the evidence and infer its meaning.

gender: the common gender: the common people.

general (noun): common people

general (adj.): of the public.

gentry: courtesy, elegance.

germane: relevant.

gib: tom-cat.

gild: supply with money.

Gis: by Gis: by Jesus.

give you: 1.1.16: God give you.

give way: allow free scope.

glimpses of the moon: fitful moonlight.

God-a-mercy: God reward you.

God buy ye: goodbye.

God dild: God reward you.

God's bodkin: God's dear body (referring to the consecrated wafer).

grace: do grace to: honour.

grainèd: ingrained, indelibly dyed.

grizzled: grey.

gross and scope: general drift.

ground: upon what ground?: from what cause?

groundling: spectator who paid one penny to stand on the playhouse floor.

gules (heraldic term): red.

gulf: whirlpool.

gyves: 4.7.21: fetters; hence, signs of criminality.

ha?: eh?

ha't: have it.

handsaw: 2.2.369: (a) carpenter's handsaw; (b) hernshaw (a bird).

handsome: stately.

hanger: strap attaching a rapier to the belt.

happily: haply, by chance.

happiness: aptness, felicity.

haps: fortunes.

harbinger: forerunner.

hard: 1.2.60: reluctant, unwilling.

hatchment: escutcheon, coat of arms.

haunt: out of haunt: out of the society of others.

have: 2.1.65, 3.2.94: understand.

haviour: behaviour, demeanour.

havoc: indiscriminate slaughter.

hawk: 2.2.369: (a) the predatory bird; (b) plasterer's tool.

head: (i: 1.1.106:) source; (ii: 4.5.101:) advancing insurrection.

health: spirit of health: angel.

hearsèd: entombed.

heavy: 3.3.84, 4.1.12: grievous, woeful.

hebona: a poison (perhaps henbane).

Hecate: goddess of Hell and witchcraft.

hectic (noun): fever.

Hecuba: Queen of Troy, wife of King Priam.

hent: 3.3.88: (a) opportunity; (b) wielding.

heraldry: (i. 1.1.87:) laws of chivalrous combat; (ii: 2.2.443:) armorial colouring.

Hercules and his load: 2.2.351: (a) Hercules, the mighty god, carrying the terrestrial globe; (b) the same as depicted on the sign of the Globe Theatre.

Herod: the King of Judea, represented in miracle plays as loudly blustering.

heyday: excitement.

hic et ubique (Latin): here and everywhere.

Hide fox, and all after!: cry uttered in a version of 'Hide and Seek'.

hobby-horse: 3.2.129: (a) dummy horse worn round the waist by mummers; (b) mummer thus attired; (c) dance performed by such a mummer.

hoist with: 3.4.206: blown up by.

home (adv.): 3.3.29: thoroughly; lay home to: upbraid thoroughly.

honest: (i: 1.5.138:) genuine; (ii: 3.1.103:) chaste; (iii: 2.2.175–7, 3.1.122): respectable.

hoodman-blind: blind man's buff.

how . . . somever: however.

hugger-mugger: secrecy.

Humorous Man: character dominated by some trait or obsession.

husbandry: thrift.

Hyperion: the sun-god.

Hyrcanian beast: tiger.

idle: (i: 2.2.137:) thoughtless;
(ii: 3.2.89: a) unoccupied; (b)
foolish; (iii: 3.4.11:) foolish.
image: likeness, representation.
impart: bestow.
impartment: communication.
impasted: formed into a paste or
crust.
impawned: staked, pledged as
security.
imperious: imperial.
implorators: solicitors
import (vb.): signify, make
known.
important: urgently importunate.
importing: concerning.
imposthume: impostume:
abscess, pus-filled boil or
swelling.
impress: enforced service.
imputation: repute.
incapable of: insensitive to.
incorporal: incorporeal, immaterial.
incorpsed: united in body.
incorrect: 1.2.95: undisciplined,
insubordinate.
indenture: **pair of indentures**:
5.1.105: deed or covenant
(binding two parties) in dupli-
cate, both copies being written
on one piece of paper which is
then divided by an irregular
cut, the irregularity aiding
subsequent verification.
index: table of contents at the
beginning of a book: hence,
prelude.
indifferent (adj.): ordinary,
neither good nor bad.
indifferent (adv.), **indifferently**:
moderately, fairly.
indirection: roundabout method.

indued: endowed.
infusion: essence.
ingenious: intelligent.
inheritor: possessor.
inhibition: 2.2.323: (a) prohibition;
(b) hindrance.
innovation: 2.2.324: (a) disorder;
(b) new fashion.
inoculate: engraft.
insinuation: ingratiation.
instance: (i: 3.2.175:) motive,
cause; (ii: 4.5.162:) token.
intil: into.
inventorially: as with a list of goods.
investments: 1.3.128: (a) vest-
ments, clothes; (b) sieges.

jealousy: suspicion.
Jephthah: judge in Israel who
sacrificed his daughter in
fulfilment of a rash vow.
jig: short entertainment (with
music and dancing) performed
after a play.
jig-maker: person (usually a
clown) who composed jigs or
performed in them.
John-a-dreams: nickname for a
dreamy fellow.
jointress: widow who holds a
jointure or life-interest.
journeyman: hired workman.
jowl (vb.): dash, hurl down.
jump (adv.): exactly.
just: 3.2.53: sound, well-balanced.

keen: 3.2.240: sharp-tongued.
keep (vb.): 2.1.8: lodge.
keep short: restrict.
kettle: kettle-drum: hollow metal
hemisphere with parchment
stretched across it.

kibe: sore on the heel.

kind: (i: 1.2.65: a) with a familial likeness; (b) kindly disposed; (ii: 4.5.146:) naturally and familially affectionate.

kindless: unnatural.

knowing: understanding.

la: interjection to add emphasis.

lapsed: 3.4.106: dilatory.

larded: bedecked, garnished.

law of writ and the liberty: 2.2.391: (probably) 'plays which obey the rules and plays which ignore them'.

lay: (i: 5.2.99:) place; (ii: 5.2.156:) stipulate; (5.2.158:) wager; **lay the odds**: wager.

laying in: burial.

lazar: leper.

lean on: depend on.

leave: 3.4.90: give up, lose.

lecture (noun): instruction.

Lenten: meagre.

let: 1.4.85: hinder.

Lethe wharf: the bank alongside Lethe, the underworld's river of forgetfulness.

level: (i: 4.1.42:) directly, straight; (ii: 4.5.151:) clear, obvious.

liberal: (i: 4.7.169:) frankly-spoken; **liberal conceit**: ample ingenuity.

lightness: 2.2.148: delirium.

limèd: trapped.

list: (i: 1.1.98, 1.2.32:) catalogue of soldiers; hence, company; (ii: 4.5.99:) boundary.

livery: (i: 1.4.32:) badge or insignia; (ii: 3.4.163, 4.7.78:) uniform denoting some rank or profession.

living: 5.1.287: (a) enduring; (b) life-like; (c) sacrificial.

lobby: passage or ante-room outside a large room.

loggats: game resembling nine-pins.

long purple: (probably) a kind of wild orchis.

luxury: lechery.

machine: mechanism of the body.

main: (i: 2.2.56:) obvious cause; (ii: 4.4.15:) main area.

mainly: 4.7.9: greatly.

malicho (from Spanish *malhecho*): mischief, wrong-doing.

margent: marginal note.

market: gainful use.

mart: traffic, bargaining.

matin: daybreak.

matter: (i: 2.2.191-3: a) subject matter; (b) topic of contention; (ii: 2.2.468:) project, intention. **Country matters**: sexual intercourse.

mazard: skull.

means: 4.5.211: manner.

meed: **in his meed**: in his pay.

mere: 5.1.274: sheer.

merely: 1.2.137: completely.

mess: meal-table.

metal: 3.2.106: (a) metal with magnetic powers; (b) mettle, temperament.

miching: sneaking, skulking.

milch: moist.

mineral (noun): 4.1.26: mine.

mo: more.

mobled: muffled: veiled or with head and face wrapped.

model: counterpart in miniature.

modesty: (i: 2.2.275:) sense of
shame; (ii: 2.2.428, 3.2.19,
5.1.198:) moderation, restraint.

moiety: portion.

mole: blemish.

monument: prodigy.

moor: expanse of marshy ground
with rank grass.

mope: be bewildered.

more above: moreover.

more and less: great and small.

moreover that: in addition to the
fact that.

mortised: tightly joined.

motion: (i: 3.4.71:) power to
move about; (ii: 4.7.100, 156:)
regulated movement.

mould: model.

mount: on mount: conspicuously.

mountebank: itinerant quack.

mouse: 3.4.182: pet-name for a
woman.

mouth (vb.): utter pompously,
declaim.

mouths: make mouths at:
grimace in derision.

muddied: confused, agitated.

muddy-mettled: thick-witted.

murdering-piece: small cannon
or mortar loaded with shrapnel.

mute (noun): actor with no
speaking part.

mutine: mutineer.

naked: destitute.

napkin: handkerchief.

native (adj.): (i: 1.2.47:) closely
related; (ii: 3.1.84:) natural.

nature: 1.2.102, 1.5.81, 3.2.379,
3.3.32, 4.5.161, 5.2.216, 229:
natural affection.

naught: improper, lewd.

nave: hub of a wheel.

Nemean lion: fierce lion killed
by Hercules.

Nero: cruel Roman emperor who
arranged the assassination of his
mother, Agrippina.

nerve: muscle, ligament.

nickname (vb.): misname.

night-gown: dressing-gown.

Niobe: legendary mother who,
when her children were slain
by the gods, wept incessantly,
even after she was turned into
stone.

nobility: 1.2.110: high degree.

noyance: harm.

nymph: beautiful young maiden
(originally, rural goddess).

obsequious: 1.2.92: dutiful in
manifesting respect for the dead.

observed of: 3.1.154: person
respected by.

occasion: opportunity.

occulted: hidden.

occurrent: occurrence.

o'er-crow: triumph over; hence,
overpower.

o'erleaven: spoil by excess.

o'er-raught: overtook.

o'er-reach: get the better of.

o'er-sizèd: painted over.

o'er-teemèd: worn out by child-
bearing.

o'ertook: 2.1.56: overcome by
drink.

offence: (i: 1.5.135-5:) offence
taken; (ii: 1.5.137, 3.2.225, 227,
3.3.56:) offensive matter;
(iii: 3.3.47): the offender.

omen: ominous event.

once: 1.5.121: ever.

open to: 2.1.30: subject to.

opposite (noun): opponent.

orbèd: spherical.

ordinant: directive.

ore: gold.

ostentation: ceremony.

outstretched: hyperbolical.

overpeer: tower above.

packing: 3.4.210: (a) away in a hurry; (b) plotting.

paddle: finger fondly.

paddock: toad.

pajock: 3.2.275: (a) patchcock (clown); (b) peacock.

pall (vb.): fail.

paragon: perfection.

pardon (noun): 1.2.56, 3.2.305: permission to depart.

parle: 1.1.62: (a) conflict; (b) dispute.

parley: 1.3.123: negotiate.

part (noun): (i: 3.2.102: a) characteristic; (b) actor's rôle; (ii: 4.7.72:) talent; (iii: 5.2.108: a) quality; (b) geographical region.

partisan: long-handled spear.

pass (noun): (i: 5.2.61:) thrust; (ii. 5.2.156:) bout of fencing. **Pass of practice**: treacherous thrust.

pass (vb.): thrust.

passage: 3.3.86, 5.2.391: death.

passages of proof: well-attested cases.

passion: 4.5.186: suffering.

patience: 3.2.104: permission.

peak (vb.): mope.

peasant (adj.): low, base.

peculiar: private.

peevish: obstinate, perverse.

pelican: bird supposed to nourish her young with her own blood.

Pelion: mountain noted in Greek mythology.

perdition: loss.

perdy: by God.

periwig-pated: bewigged.

perpend: ponder.

petar (cf. Spanish *petar* or French *pétard*): mine, bomb.

phrase: 2.2.431: phraseology, language.

picked: 5.1.132: fastidious, finical.

pickers and stealers: hands.

picture in little: miniature.

pigeon-livered: meek.

pioner: sapper, military digger.

pitch (noun): literally, height from which a falcon swoops; hence, lofty aim.

platform: terrace.

plausive: pleasing.

pleurisy: disease thought to be caused by excess of blood.

pocky: infected with pox (syphilis).

point: **at point exactly**: in every particular.

Polack: 2.2.63: Polish King.

Polacks: 1.1.63: Polish warriors.

Pole: Pole Star.

politic: 4.3.20: (a) cunning; (b) busy in statecraft.

porpentine: porcupine.

posset (vb.): curdle.

posy: short motto.

powers: 4.4.9: troops.

practice: (i: 2.2.38:) action; (ii: 4.7.66, 5.2.311:) stratagem, plot; **of practice**: 4.7.137: treacherous.

precurse: heralding.

pregnant: (i: 2.2.205:) full of meaning, apt; (ii: 3.2.60:) readily moved.

prescript: precept.

present: 5.1.285: immediate.

presently: at once.

pressure: image, impress.

prevent: anticipate.

pricked on: spurred on.

primal: original.

primy: in its prime or springtime.

privates: 2.2.230: (a) ordinary subjects without rank or office; (b) genitalia.

probation: proof.

process: (i: 1.5.37:) story; (ii: 3.3.29:) proceedings; (iii: 4.3.64:) mandate.

progress: ceremonial journey.

pronounce: (i: 2.2.498:) proclaim; (ii: 3.2.298:) deliver a statement.

proof: (i: 2.2.477:) proven strength; (ii: 3.4.37:) impenetrable. **Passages of proof:** confirmatory instances.

proper: (i: 2.1.111:) natural; (ii: 5.2.66:) own, very.

property: (i: 2.1.100, 5.1.65:) nature, characteristic quality; (ii: 2.2.554: a) essential quality; (b) possessions.

proportions: 1.2.32: forces.

provincial rose: rosette resembling a French rose (probably of Provence).

puffed: (i: 1.3.49:) bloated; (ii: 4.4.49:) exalted.

purgation: (i: 3.2.295: a) purging of the body; (b) confession.

purging: (i: 2.2.196): exuding; (ii: 3.3.85): cleansing.

pursy: short-winded; hence, out of condition.

push: present push: immediate action.

put on: (i: 1.3.94:) impress upon; (ii: 2.1.19:) impose on; (iii: 4.7.130, 5.2.376:) instigate; (iv: 5.2.390:) put to the test.

put one from: remove, separate.

Pyrrhus: vengeful son of Achilles.

quaintly: artfully.

quality: profession.

quantity: (i: 3.2.160:) proportion; (ii: 3.4.74:) modicum; (iii: 5.1.260:) amount.

quarry: 5.2.357: literally, heap of slain deer after a hunt; hence, large number of corpses.

quest: inquest.

question (noun): (i: 1.1.111, 5.2.368:) topic; (ii: 2.2.331:) controversy; (iii: 3.1.13:) conversation.

questionable: question-provoking.

quiddity (from *quidditas*, the distinctive nature of an entity): abstruse distinction.

quietus: discharge of a debt, settlement of an account.

quillity: abstruse distinction..

quintessence: utmost refinement.

quit: 5.2.254: draw level.

quote: note, observe.

rack: clouds in the upper air driven before the wind.

rank: gross, excessive; **ranker:** higher.

ravel out: disentangle.

rawer: 5.2.119: crude, unskilled.

razed: slit, slashed.

reach (noun): capacity.

reck (vb.): heed.

reckon: 2.2.120: (a) count; (b) express in verse.

recognizance: bond acknowledging a debt or obligation.

recorder: wind instrument with holes for fingering.

recover the wind of: get to windward of (so that the quarry, scenting the hunter, runs into a net or ambush).

recovery: 5.1.101: (a) lawsuit to obtain possession of an estate; (b) attainment, outcome.

rede: counsel, advice.

reechy: foul-smelling.

reels: 1.4.9: (i, vb.:) dances wildly; (ii, noun:) revels.

regard (noun): consideration, estimation.

region (noun): open air, sky; (adj.) in the sky.

relative: relevant.

relish (noun): trace.

relish (vb.): retain a trace.

remiss: careless.

remorse: 2.2.478: compassion.

removed: remote.

replication: reply.

repugnant: refractory.

requiem: song or chant for the repose of the dead.

resolute (noun): determined person.

resolve (vb.): dissolve.

respect (noun): consideration.

responsive to: appropriate to, suitable for.

retrograde: contrary, opposed.

revolution: alteration, change produced by time.

rhapsody: confused mixture.

Rhenish: wine from the Rhineland.

rheum: watery discharge, particularly tears.

ring: cracked within the ring: 2.2.416: (a) no longer legal tender, like a coin cracked or clipped within the circle round the monarch's head; (b, of a boy's voice) broken, and thus useless for female rôles.

rival: partner.

robustious: boisterous.

rood: by the rood: by Christ's cross.

Roscius: famous Roman actor.

rose: (i: 3.1.152:) paragon, perfection; (ii: 3.4.41:) emblem of ideal love. **Rose of May**: youthful beauty.

round (adv.): 2.2.138: directly.

round (adj.): 3.1.183, 3.4.5: straightforward, direct.

rouse: (i: 1.2.127:) bumper: full cup or glass for drinking a toast; (ii: 1.4.8, 2.1.56:) carousal, drinking bout.

row: 2.2.407: stanza.

rub (noun): impediment, obstacle.

rummage: bustle, turmoil.

sables: (i: 3.2.125: a) expensive furs; (b) black mourning garments; (ii: 4.7.79:) fur garments for old men.

sage: grave, solemn.

sallets: tasty morsels (perhaps ribaldries).

sanity: 1.3.21: well-being, health.

sans (from French): without.

sat on: 5.1.4: conducted an inquest on.

satyr: goat-legged companion of Bacchus, god of wine and revelry.

savoury: appetising.

saw: 1.5.100: maxim, saying.

scape: escape.

sconce: head.

scorn: 3.2.23: object of scorn.

scrimer (cf. French *escrimeur*): fencer.

scruple: 4.4.40: (a) scrupulous habit; (b) tiny amount.

scullion: kitchen menial.

sea-gown: high-collared, short-sleeved gown, worn by seamen.

season: (i: 1.2.192, 2.1.28:) temper, moderate; (ii: 1.3.81, 3.2.202:) ripen, bring to maturity; (iii: 3.3.86:) prepare.

secure (adj.): unguarded, unsuspecting.

seeming (noun): appearance, aspect.

seized of: possessed of.

semblable (noun): likeness.

sense: 3.4.37, 70, 160: feeling, sensibility.

sensible and true avouch: reliable evidence provided by one of the five senses.

sensibly: feelingly, acutely.

'se offendendo': phrase confused with 'se defendendo', a plea of self-defence.

sergeant: 5.2.329: officer of a court with power to arrest people.

service: (i: 1.3.13: a) allegiance; (b) religious service; (ii: 4.3.23:) course in a meal.

set (vb.): (1.4.65:) value, estimate; (ii: 3.4.60:) imprint.

shape: (i: 1.4.43, 1.5.54:) form; (i: 4.7.88:) attitude, posture; (iii: 4.7.149:) rôle.

shard: fragment of earthenware.

shark up: gather rapidly and indiscriminately.

shent: put to shame.

showing: **great showing**: distinguished appearance.

shreds and patches: ragged and patched clothing.

shuffled off: sloughed off, cast off.

siege: rank, status.

skirts: outlying parts.

slander (vb.): disgrace.

sledded: 1.1.63: on sledges. (See, however, the note to 1.1.63 on p. 153.)

sling: 3.1.58: strap from which a missile is hurled.

sliver: withy: slender flexible branch.

softly: 4.4.8: (a) quietly; (b) slowly; (c) steadily.

solicit: incite, prompt.

sort (vb.): accord, be fitting.

sphere: one of the concentric and transparent hollow globes which supposedly revolved round the earth and bore the planets and stars.

spill: kill.

splenative: splenetic, liable to fits of anger.

springe: snare.

stained: 4.4.57: dishonoured.

stand me now upon: put an obligation on me now.

star: (i: 1.4.32: a) destiny; (b) distinctive mark; (ii: 2.2.140:) destined place.

state: (i: 1.1.101, 1.2.20:) government; (ii: 2.2.498:) rule, power.

station: bearing, stance.

statist: statesman.

statute: legal bond making a debtor's land the security.

stay upon your patience: await your permission.

stick off: show to advantage.

still (adv.): constantly, always.

stithy: forge, smithy.

stomach: 1.1.100: (a) appetite; (b) ambition.

stop (noun): finger-hole in a wind instrument.

stoup: drinking-vessel.

straight: 2.2.419, 5.1.3: at once.

strewments: flowers strewn on a grave.

strike (vb.): 1.1.162: destroy by evil influence.

stuck: 4.7.160: thrust, lunge.

subject: 1.1.72, 1.2.33: subjects, people.

sun: in the sun: (i: 1.2.67: a) in the sunshine of royal favour; (b) in the rôle of son (to Claudius); (ii: 2.2.183: a) in sunshine; (b) close to royalty, namely the Prince.

supervise (noun): first reading.

suppliance: pastime, diversion.

sweep my way: clear my path.

swoopstake (version of 'sweepstake'): taking all the stakes in a game at once.

Switzers: door-guards, beadles; not necessarily Swiss.

table: 1.5.98, 107: writing-tablet used as notebook. **Table-book:** book of writing-tablets.

take: 1.1.163: bewitch.

target: light shield.

tar (vb.): incite.

tax: censure; **tax him home:** rebuke him soundly.

Tellus: goddess of the earth.

tempered: mixed, concocted.

tenable: retained.

tend: attend, wait in readiness.

tender (adj.): youthful.

tender (vb.): (i: 1.3.107, 4.3.39:) have regard for; (ii: 1.3.109:) render to.

tent: probe.

Termagant: noisy fiendish character in Mystery Plays.

terms: 3.3.5, 4.7.26: condition.

tetter: eruption of the skin.

thought: 3.1.85, 4.5.186: melancholy reflection.

thrift: (i: 1.2.180:) prudent economy; (ii: 3.2.61) profit.

through and through: straight through.

tickle o'th'sere: quick to respond.

time: (i: 3.1.114:) present age; (ii: 4.7.110, 148:) circumstance.

tinct: colour.

tithe: tenth part.

to: 1.2.139, 3.1.52: compared with.

toil (noun): net, snare.

too too: far too.

top: in the top of mine: with greater authority than mine; **on the top of question:** with the maximum of contention.

touch: 3.2.344: fingering of a musical instrument.

touched: 4.5.205: tainted, touched with guilt.

toward: impending.

toy (noun): idle fancy, trifle.

trace (vb.): follow his tracks.

trade: business.

trick (noun): (i: 4.4.61:) trifle, brief spell; (ii: 4.7.186:) way; (iii: 4.5.5, 5.1.95:) trickery; (iv: 5.1.86:) knack.

tricked: 2.2.444: literally, with colours schematically indicated: hence, marked.

trophy: memorial.

tropically: figuratively, metaphorically.

truepenny: trusty fellow.

trumpet: trumpeter.

truncheon: staff of office.

truster: one who believes or credits.

try conclusions: experiment.

tune of the time: fashionable tone.

turn the beam: turn the scale, preponderate.

turn Turk with: 3.2.267: become a renegade to, desert.

tyrannically: vehemently.

tyrannous: pitilessly harsh.

umbrage: shadow.

unaneled: unanointed, without extreme unction.

unbated: not blunted.

unbraced: unfastened.

uncharge: 4.7.66: exonerate.

unction: ointment.

uncurrent: unacceptable, invalid.

undergo: support.

uneffectual: losing its effect.

unfellowed: unmatched, unequalled.

unfold: disclose, declare.

ungalled: ungrazed, unharmed.

ungracious: ungodly.

unhouseled: without the Eucharist.

unimprovèd: 1.1.96: (a) unrestrained; (b) unrebuked.

union: large pearl of high value.

unkennel: reveal.

unpregnant of: not committed to.

unprevailing: unavailing.

unproportioned: inordinate.

unreclaimed: untamed.

unshaped: confused.

unsifted: untested, inexperienced.

unsinewed: weak, feeble.

unvalued: worthless.

unwrung: unharmed.

unyoke: finish.

upshot: issue, conclusion.

upspring: 1.4.9: (i, adj.:) upstart, newly come into fashion; (ii, noun:) dance or dance-step.

use (noun): (i: 1.2.134:) usage, way; (ii: 3.4.162:) practice.

usurp: (i: 1.1.46:) invade, appropriate; (ii: 3.2.251:) encroach.

vail: lower.

valanced: fringed with hangings.

validity: strength.

vantage: of vantage: (3.3.33: i) in addition; (ii) from an advantageous position.

variable: 3.1.172: diverse, various; **variable service**: different courses of food.

ventage: finger-hole in a windinstrument.

Vice: clownish character who, in a Morality play, represented one of the human vices.

videlicet (Latin): that is to say, namely.

virtue: (i: 1.3.16:) integrity, purity; (ii: 4.5.155:) power.

voice: (i: 1.3.23, 1.3.28, 5.2.349:) approval, nomination; (ii: 5.2.234:) pronouncement.

vouch: guarantee.

voucher and **double voucher**: process of summoning a guarantor (or second guarantor) of a person's entitlement.

Vulcan: Roman fire-god, smith and armourer.

vulgar: (i: 1.2.99:) commonplace, obvious; (1.3.61:) common, low in manner.

wag: 5.1.257: move.

wait upon: attend.

wake: 1.4.8: stay up late.

wand'ring star: planet.

wanton: 5.2.292: (probably) spoilt child.

war'nt: warrant, guarantee; of **warrant**: guaranteed.

wassail: drinking of toasts, carousal.

waste: 1.2.198: (a) desolate time; (b) waist: middle.

watch (noun): 2.2.147: insomnia, sleeplessness.

water-fly: (perhaps: i) dragon-fly; (ii) midge.

weeds: (i: 4.7.79:) garments; (ii: 4.7.171:) wild flowers.

wharf: bank of a river.

wheel: 4.5.171: burden, refrain: part of a song repeated at the end of every stanza.

windlass: roundabout course.

winnowed: refined.

wit: (i: 2.2.90:) intelligent utterance; (ii: 3.2.309:) mind.

witching time: time for witchcraft.

withers: part of the back between the shoulder-blades.

wonder (noun): (i: 4.5.87:) bewilderment; (ii: 5.2.356:) wretchedness.

woodcock: bird supposed to be easily caught in a snare.

woo't: wilt (thou).

word: (i: 1.5.110:) motto; (ii: 4.5.105:) promise, pledge.

work: 1.1.67: pursue mentally.

working: 2.2.136, 538: activity.

wrack (vb.): ruin, seduce.

yaw: deviate from course.

yeasty: frothy, superficial.

yielding: consent.

zone: **burning zone**: orbit in which the sun moves.